# A Place for Children

Public libraries as a major force in
children's reading

# A Place for Children

## Public libraries as a major force in children's reading

British Library Research and Innovation Report 117

Edited by

## Judith Elkin
Dean of Faculty of Computing, Information and English
University of Central England in Birmingham

## Margaret Kinnell
Dean of Faculty of Science, Loughborough University

With contributions from
**Debbie Denham, Peggy Heeks and Ray Lonsdale**

Library Association Publishing
London

Published by
Library Association Publishing
7 Ridgmount Street
London WC1E 7AE

Library Association Publishing is wholly owned by The Library Association.

First published 2000

British Library Cataloguing in Publication Data
A catalogue record for this book is available from the British Library.

RIC/G/340
ISSN 1366-8218
ISBN 1-85604-320-7

Typeset in 10/13pt Jenson Recut and 12/13pt Franklin Gothic from authors' disks by Library Association Publishing.
Printed and made in Great Britain by Bookcraft (Bath) Ltd, Midsomer Norton, Somerset.

This book is dedicated to all the library authorities, librarians, teachers, parents and children who took part in this research and continue to believe in the power of libraries to transform lives.

# Contents

# The contributors

**Debbie Denham** BLib CertEd ALA is a Senior Lecturer in the School of Information Studies at the University of Central England in Birmingham. She previously worked as a public librarian specializing in work with children and as a school librarian. Her teaching and research centre on the field of children's literature and librarianship. Recently completed projects and reports include research for Book Trust concerning widening access to information about children's books and a national survey of the range of IT facilities and services available for use by children in public libraries. Debbie is joint editor, with Judith Elkin, of the *New Review of Children's Literature and Librarianship*.

**Professor Judith Elkin** BA PhD FLA MIInfSc is Dean of the Faculty of Computing, Information and English at the University of Central England in Birmingham. She is a member of the Library and Information Commission and Chair of the Higher Education Funding Council's Research Assessment Exercise for 2001. She was previously Head of Chidren's Library Services for Birmingham Public Libraries and has researched widely in the field of children's libraries and children's and multicultural literature. Her most recent books are *Focus on the Child: libraries, literature and learning* (with Ray Lonsdale, Library Association Publishing 1996, and *The Puffin book of twentieth century children's literature* (Puffin, 1999).

**Margaret Kinnell Evans** BA MBA PhD PGCE FIInfSc FLA is Professor of Information Studies in the Department of Information Science, Loughborough University, where she is also Dean of the Faculty of Science and Director of Information Strategy and Services. She has researched widely in the fields of public sector information services, and childhood and children's literature. Recent books include *Continuity and innovation in the public library* (with Paul Sturges, Library Association Publishing, 1996 and *Marketing in the non-profit sector* (with J. MacDougall, Butterworth Heinemann, 1997). She has also published numerous scholarly articles and given many invited conference presentations in the UK and overseas.

**Dr Peggy Heeks** MA FLA has had a long association with children's and school libraries, firstly as Senior Assistant County Librarian for Berkshire and latterly through research undertaken at Oxford and Loughborough Universities. Committee work has included chairing of the Library Association/School Library Association Joint Standing Committee, and service as a governor of the Children's Book Foundation. Peggy Heeks is a Research Fellow in the Department of Information Science, Loughborough University. Recent books and reports include: *Learning support for special educational needs* (Taylor-Graham), *Public libraries and the arts* (Library Association) and *School library services today* (British Library). She has also published numerous articles in scholarly and professional journals.

**Ray Lonsdale** MA ALA is a Senior Lecturer in the Department of Information and Library Studies, The University of Wales Aberystwyth, where he is responsible for teaching and research in the fields of children's librarianship and children's literature. He was previously Assistant Principal Librarian for Education and Youth Library Services in Knowsley Metropolitan Library Service. He has published widely in academic and professional journals, and co-authored the book *Focus on the child: libraries, literacy and learning* with Judith Elkin. This year he was appointed Editor of the *The School Librarian*. For the past 20 years he has acted as an international consultant in information and library science for the British Council, the World Bank, the Overseas Development Administration and a number of foreign governments.

# Introduction
## Children's libraries for the next millennium

Judith Elkin and Margaret Kinnell

We always want to keep coming back. (Sarah, aged 5)

Supporting children's libraries in their focus as a place for every child was the motivation for this book. It is based upon a major piece of national research into the relationship between children's reading and public libraries. We began with the view that library services for children and young people were a key national asset in supporting children's reading needs, and a tremendous resource unlike any other. Public libraries have been, and will continue to be, places for children, with materials and professional expertise that uniquely enable children and young people to unlock the door to their reading and hence to their social, intellectual and emotional development. However, in undertaking this study we considered that library roles and functions in supporting children's reading required refocusing in the light of a whole range of influences. Library services, like all other public services, are having to face the effects of many changes both to society at large and to their own operating environment.

The research was focused in the UK but the editors believe that the research findings, the good practice identified and the vision of libraries for the future, are relevant world-wide. All countries face change and libraries, as part of a political, cultural and educational framework, face threats from the economy and from technology. Librarians everywhere must be prepared to accommodate change flexibly, creatively and innovatively.

## A Place for Children

The Place for Children project was unique in its coverage, investigating the qualitative impact of public libraries on children's reading, and identifying the benefits and effectiveness of service provision, UK-wide. It was funded by the British Library Research and Innovation Centre from the end of 1996 to 1998, with supporting funding for a case study from the Library and Information Services Council (Northern Ireland). We were aiming to deal with two broad questions:

- how children and young people's lifestyles and expectations were changing and how public libraries were responding or should respond to these
- how to improve the management of children's public library services to meet these new needs as well as to maintain the continuity of services.

The research attempted to:

- assess how significant the public library was continuing to be in supporting the reading development of children and young people from birth through to 16
- produce service criteria and performance indicators which could be used to inform future directions and policy decisions.

A Place for Children was not only the result of work undertaken during the project. It also included the collective experience of a team, from the University of Central England in Birmingham, Loughborough University and the University of Wales, Aberystwyth. Key members of the research team have contributed over many years to the field of children and young people's librarianship.

In focusing our study on public libraries' roles in supporting children's reading, we emphasized that reading development was key to children's success in their education and also in wider emotional and social terms. The special, indeed unique, place of the public library in meeting these needs gave us the title for the study.

## The need for research

More than 111 million children's books were borrowed from UK public libraries in 1995/6. Overall, use of the service is increasing. The public library provides the only statutory local government service available to children from babyhood to adolescence. Yet there has never been a national assessment of its value. The research team identified a need for a major empirical study that would investigate the role of public libraries in supporting children's reading development. The project was, therefore, designed to embrace children's acquisition of initial and higher-level skills, their access to literature and information sources in fiction and non-fiction, the implications of the new literacies now required by young people in a multimedia environment, and the multicultural environment of many local authorities. The study sought to identify those criteria which make for excellence in services which also foster reading and enhance access by young people. It also assessed strategies for service development.

This was a particularly apposite time to undertake the investigation, given the LISC Report *Investing in children* (1995) and Aslib's *Review of public library services in England and Wales*:

We recognise the vital part that public libraries play in supporting reading and developing information literacy in the lives of children and young people. (Aslib, 1995, 193)

These thoughts were echoed in the Government's response to the Aslib report:

Libraries provide an important opportunity for young children to develop reading and a love of books, the first rung on the ladder to literacy and learning throughout life . . . Young children's experience of books and stories is known to have a considerable impact on their future educational attainment. (Department of National Heritage, 1997, 20)

Literacy and the development of reading skills have also become a priority for the current UK Government and have been given a fresh focus in the Government-funded Year of Reading 1998–1999.

## Research issues

As was identified, though, in *Focus on the child* (Elkin and Lonsdale, 1996), there was a need not just to look at the negative aspects of cuts in service provision but to highlight good practice, to emphasize opportunities for growth and to identify the scale of the investment that was required. While the LISU surveys had shown that a major issue for all public library services was the effect of government cutbacks and local government reorganization on public library services for children, there was also the question of the impact of educational change on public and school library services. How the relationship between these two elements of services for children and young people should be managed was a key issue.

A further major issue was the continuing role of the book and how books were to be promoted by public library services alongside all the other literacies that children would need. The technological age demands greater sophistication from information users – visual literacy as well as advanced electronic navigation skills, and more highly developed traditional literacy skills. The book remains, and will remain, of vital importance in all of this, as well as providing children with the emotional, intellectual and social support that they need.

## Library and Information Statistics Unit surveys

The fullest of the ongoing statistically based studies are those published by the Library and Information Statistics Unit (LISU), which have enabled trend analyses that indicate the state of public library services for children in terms of the services provided, charges, stock, staffing and expenditure. However, the LISU surveys raise as many questions as can be answered from a statistical survey. The 1997/8 survey indicates, for example, that levels of professional staff in services continue to fall, with the worst provision found in Wales and the English unitary authorities. On average, there was just one professional children's librarian for every 16,000 children in these areas during the past five years, whilst there was one librarian to 7,000 children in the London boroughs. And some 10% of public library authorities employ no specialist children's staff at all. Also of concern is the low spend on materials. The English metropolitan districts have preserved spending the most, but spending in Wales has fallen steadily over the past five years, and in all types of authority other than the metropolitan districts materials spending per capita in cash terms was lower in 1997/8 than in 1992/3. These figures indicate a real problem as to how public libraries can continue to support literacy and reading development when both staffing and materials are at such a low ebb. Issues are in decline for children – in the metropolitan districts a steady fall of 28% is recorded over the five-year period – which underlines the need for greater investment and the best use of resources to maximize the impact of library services.

Statistics such as these paint the picture for the whole sector and help in mapping the extent of the resourcing problem facing public libraries. What was also needed, though, was an extensive analysis of the situation across the UK in terms of the range and depth of services being offered to support children's reading development and the contexts in which they were being delivered. Given the problems of resourcing services, evidence of good practice was also needed, to ensure that service excellence could be promoted nationally – and indeed internationally. Children's reading needs are universally important.

## Social and demographic change

The first question posed by the Place for Children research was this: children's and young people's lives, lifestyles and expectations have changed; how have public libraries responded to that change? The vision and philosophy of the public library as a community resource clearly need to evolve in parallel to meet new needs. Within the overall trend towards an ageing population, the 0–16 age group is increasing slightly, with projections that it will rise to 20.7% of the total by 2001, from 20.3% in 1991. The proportion of children from black and ethnic minority groups is much higher than the proportion in the population as a whole. Further aspects of UK society today include many religious faiths contrasting with growing secularization, increased Europeanization, and multiculturalism and international awareness in a rapidly shrinking world. Young people now travel more widely and frequently than any previous generation. Family life in the UK also manifests many of the effects of change. Approximately 30% of marriages now end in divorce, with a consequent growth in the number of single-parent families. It is estimated that by the year 2000 25% of children will be born to unmarried women, and that less than 30% of adolescents will have lived in a continuously intact family through all 18 years of their youth (Aslib, 1995, 53). Long-term unemployment and poverty still characterize many areas of the country, and some research suggests that the poor are becoming poorer (Oppenheim and Harker, 1996). These trends affect social stability and bring additional demands to a number of public services, including libraries. Rather ironically, at a time of breakdown in family life, we see a new emphasis on community life and agencies of community regeneration. This, in turn, brings calls for greater collaboration between these organizations. A study funded by the Gulbenkian Foundation has proposed developing parliamentary structures to ensure that central government is more responsive to the needs of children, in recognition of these social changes (Hodgkin and Newell, 1996).

## Children

Children's life experiences and expectations are therefore similar to, and yet at the same time very different from, those of the previous generation. The social context has undergone rapid changes and yet children remain as individuals who defy categorization. The child may be seen as all or any of the following:

- thinker
- carer, concerned at what is going on in the world, and often politically aware
- campaigner: for animal rights; feminist issues; gay rights; anti-nuclear issues; peace and conservation
- coping with growing up: sibling rivalry; adolescence; broken home; child abuse; drugs; unemployment and an uncertain future
- handling insecurity at home, at school, in society at large
- living in a society where the role of the child is unclear and the environment insecure
- threatened by increasing violence on the streets, as well as in rural areas
- meeting new emotions, new relationships, coping with the realities of life, of survival and death
- growing up in a world increasingly dominated by technology, influenced by radio, television, video and multimedia, and increasingly able to access the uncharted and largely uncontrolled wastes of the information superhighway through the Internet. (Elkin and Lonsdale, 1996, 2–3)

## Management to meet change

The second question posed by the research was how to improve the management of children's public library services to meet these new needs as well as maintaining the continuity of service. It was essential to have not only a vision of what could and should be achieved, but also the means to translate ideas and aspirations into operational realities.

The type of change being encountered in the present work environment is particularly challenging, intense in its pace and involving situations to which traditional professional solutions no longer apply. 'We are working at a time when concepts of organization and leadership are in full ferment. The assumptions that led to the success of the bureaucratic model are disintegrating. A collective effort is under way to redefine how work is done and how our organizations are led.' (Spears, 1998, 333) There is evidence of the shift in both management literature and practice. Once, management manuals set out confidently the series of steps needed to deal with change, moving from initiation, through implementation to integration. 'New' management takes a very different approach, proceeding by intuition as much as analysis. It is significant that one of the best-selling management titles of the decade is called *Thriving on chaos* (Peters, 1989) and that advertisements for executive posts call for risk-taking and entrepreneurial qualities. The increase in the pace of change means that managers must expect turbulence rather than stability.

This brings fresh challenges in using the workforce to maximum effect. Advice abounds. An increase of 288% in the number of management books published between 1973 and 1993 in the UK has been identified (Line, 1995). Over the period, work patterns have become more flexible and interest in holistic management has grown. This has resulted in successful organizations approaching the task of management by exploiting *all* of the available techniques to support the optimal use of diminishing resources.

## Children's reading and the public library

Concern for children's reading development and their reading and informational needs has been expressed over many years in numerous government reports, the writings of educationalists and library and information specialists. Of particular note were: The Bullock Report (Department of Education and Science, 1975); The Kingman Report (Department of Education and Science, 1988); *Children and their books* (Whitehead et al, 1977); the Scottish Arts Council's *Readership report* (Working Party, 1989). Such reports have been complemented by educationalists such as Wells (1982), Protherough (1989) and Meek (1991), and library and information specialists such as Marshall (1975 and 1982), Heather (1981) and Kinnell (1991).

Despite the considerable research which has been undertaken into children's and young people's reading within the education sector, the relationship between public libraries and children's reading has been largely neglected. For the most part, studies have focused on links between the home, schools and reading development. Research conducted by the National Centre for Children's Literature (NCRCL) at Roehampton, which investigated children's reading habits through surveys and interviews in schools, confirmed the continuing popularity and cultural significance of books to children (Roehampton Institute, 1994). A gap existed, however, in the area of support for children's reading through the public library service – a dimension excluded from the NCRCL investigation.

## Public library manifesto

At the international level, the UNESCO *Public library manifesto* recognized that:

> The public library, the local gateway to knowledge, provides a basic condition for lifelong learning, independent decision-making and cultural development of the individual and social groups. The Manifesto proclaims UNESCO's belief in the public library as a living force for education, culture and information, and as an essential agent for the fostering of peace and spiritual welfare through the minds of men and women. (IFLA, 1995)

Among the key missions which the Manifesto relates to information, literacy, education and culture are:

- creating and strengthening reading habits in children from an early age
- supporting both individual and self-conducted education at all levels
- providing opportunities for personal creative development
- stimulating the imagination and creativity of children and young people
- promoting awareness of cultural heritage
- fostering intercultural dialogue and favouring cultural diversity
- facilitating the development of information and computer literacy skills
- supporting and participating in literacy activities and programmes for all age groups, and initiating such activities if necessary.

In the UK much has been achieved by British public library authorities in delivering quality services; UK services to teenagers and pre-school children, in particular, are amongst the most innovative in the world. There has been support from The Library Association through its published guidelines, *Children and young people* (Blanshard, 1997), and through the seminal text *Focus on the child* (Elkin and Lonsdale, 1996).

## Children and young people

The Library Association guidelines *Children and young people* (Blanshard, 1997) spelt out the role of the children's library in considerable detail and established a sound framework for considering services to children and young people. They began by identifying four areas of child development where books and stories and, implicitly, libraries were vitally important:

- **intellectual and emotional development**
- **language development** – particularly crucial in the pre-school years, and an area where the library can enhance the partnership between parent, child and teacher
- **social development** – children's attitudes to one another and to society are significantly shaped by reading
- **education development** – the need for children to acquire reading and information skills is now being reinforced throughout the curriculum. (Blanshard, 1977)

## Focus on the child

*Focus on the child: libraries, literacy and learning* (Elkin and Lonsdale, 1996) provided a critical analysis of library services to young people in the UK, assessing the degree to which they were responding to the contemporary needs of the child and the forces of change presented by society. It set out to provide a broad conceptual framework and philosophical approach for students and practitioners. The starting point for *Focus on the child*, as the title suggested, focused on the child and the child's needs in the way of books and other materials to support literacy and learning. The premise was taken that reading and books played an important part in the child's personal development and education, and that access to books through libraries, and the role of libraries in supporting the child's learning and early literacy, can help to prepare children for life in an uncertain and changing world.

As Elkin said elsewhere:

Children are complex individuals growing up in a rapidly changing world. Books and literacy are important for early development and lifelong learning, even in today's technological age. Early exposure to stories and to books is an essential part of the child's pre-school and pre-reading experience and needs reinforcing as they become sophisticated readers, learners and thinkers. Early access to books is vital, to encourage wide, diverse reading and to help children to understand the enormous pleasure and excitement to be gained from reading and learning, even in the age of the computer. Books open new worlds, as an old Chinese proverb sums up nicely: 'A book is like a garden that can be carried in the pocket.' The role of libraries is important in supporting the child's diverse reading and ensuring everyone has access to as wide a range of books as possible: no one individual can afford to own the range of books that a library can provide. Libraries, both in schools and in public libraries, contribute to children's leisure needs as well as their intellectual, emotional, social and educational and language development. The public library fulfils a complementary social function through its programmes of storyhours and activities, providing a bright, welcoming, attractive and safe place for children to browse, to read, to study, to meet other children. (Elkin, 1998)

Beyond *Focus on the child* and its analysis of current issues in children's librarianship, there has been little documentation of practice. Some small-scale but potentially significant local initiatives are being undertaken to promote reading and the use of information but they go largely unrecorded. There is a marked paucity of comparative investigations between authorities and, more importantly, there has been little in the way of empirical research to document service activities and to gauge their impact on children's reading. This omission was identified by the Library and Information Services Council (England) Working Party report *Investing in children* (1995), which investigated children's reading in the context of overall public library service development and reaffirmed the critical role which the public library plays in supporting children's reading development.

## Investing in children

The Library and Information Services Council (England) Working Party on Library Services for Children and Young People had gathered evidence from a wide range of interested parties, although Scotland was not represented, which diminished the national validity of the report. The most valuable function of the report was to highlight the need for central and local government to develop policy and provide resources to strengthen the work of public libraries:

> . . . it is our clear view that, at a time when unfulfilled reading potential affects the economic, cultural and social life of the country, the potential of a library, and in particular the public library which is freely available to all, as a force in support of reading and information literacy cannot be too strongly emphasised. (LISC(E), 1995, 16)

There were 20 specific recommendations from the findings, ranging from the need for local authorities to publish integrated strategies for children and young people's library and information services, to the development of model standards for services. The report also acknowledged the paucity of research data on the impact of public libraries on children's reading and their ways of working with children. The case studies which the report had identified simply whetted the appetite for more in-depth analysis of what was happening across all the countries of the UK in order to show how exactly children's services might best be improved. The report concluded that the impacts and benefits of library services should therefore 'be explored through well-constructed research, complemented by studies that approach the issues from the child's perspective.' (LISC(E), 1995, 17)

A Place for Children research can be seen as a response to this concern.

## A Place for Children: the book

The stage having been set here, Chapter 1 goes on to consider in more depth the service context facing library services for children. The findings of this study are related to the wider environment at national as well as local level. In Chapter 2 the purposes of services for children are discussed. These take into account new demands as well as the important continuities for which library services are rightly cherished. Chapter 3 is concerned with assessing clients' needs in depth, taking account of all the clients concerned with children's services: parents, carers, teachers as well as children. In Chapter 4 the important issues surrounding collection development to meet changing needs are discussed. Materials now include all media, and managing their selection, acquisition, distribution, organization and accessibility is a major concern. The promotion of library services to meet clients' needs, and to ensure the continuing visibility of the service against competing demands, is discussed in Chapter 5. Promotion includes consideration of innovative programmes in authorities. In Chapter 6 the vexed question of assessment of services is discussed, setting the findings of this study against a range of work that has been undertaken on the management of performance in public library services. In Chapter 7 we offer our overview of the current state of libraries for children in the UK, with conclusions and recommendations for future actions to move services forward. All quotes from the case studies appear in italics. Quotes from other sources are not italicized.

The editors would like to thank the researchers who participated in the research and everyone who gave their time willingly, either to be interviewed as a member of a focus group or to take part in the steering committee. We would also like to reiterate that, whilst much of the evidence presented in each chapter, and particularly the good practice, is UK-based, we believe that it is highly relevant far beyond the United Kingdom.

## References

Aslib (1995) *Review of the public library service in England and Wales for the Department of National Heritage*, Aslib.

Blanshard, C (1997) *Children and young people: Library Association guidelines for public library services*, 2nd edn, Library Association Publishing.

Creaser, C and Murphy, A (1997) *A survey of library services to schools and children in the UK 1996–97*, Library and Information Statistics Unit.

Creaser, C and Murphy, A (1998) *A survey of library services to schools and children in the UK 1997–8*, Library and Information Statistics Unit.

Department of Education and Science (1975) *A language for life*, The Bullock Report, HMSO.

Department of Education and Science (1988) *Report of the committee of enquiry into the teaching of English language*, The Kingman Report, HMSO.

Department of National Heritage (1997) *Reading the future: a review of public libraries in England*, DNH.

Elkin, J (1998) Focus on the child: children's libraries in Portugal: report of a workshop held in Lisbon during the Festival of Public Libraries, *The New Review of Children's Literature and Librarianship*, **4**, 93–106.

Elkin, J and Lonsdale, R (1996) *Focus on the child: libraries, literacy and learning*, Library Association Publishing.

Heather, P (1981) *Young people's reading: a study of the leisure reading of 13–15 year-olds*, University of Sheffield Centre for Research on User Studies.

Hodgkin, R and Newell, P (1996) *Effective government structures for children*, Calouste Gulbenkian Foundation.

IFLA (International Federation of Library Associations) (1995) *UNESCO Public library manifesto*, IFLA.

Kinnell, M (1991) *Managing fiction in libraries*, Library Association Publishing.

Library and Information Services Council (England) Working Party on Library Services for Children and Young People (1995) *Investing in children: the future of library services for children and young people*, Library and Information Series 22, HMSO.

Line, M B (1995) Needed: a pathway through the swamp of management literature, *Library Management*, 16 (1), 36–8.

Marshall, M (1975) *Libraries and literature for teenagers*, Deutsch.

Marshall, M (1982) *The state of public library services to teenagers in Britain 1981*, Library and Information Research Report 5, British Library.

Meek, M (1991) *On being literate*, Bodley Head.

Oppenheim, C and Harker, L (1996) *Poverty: the facts*, Child Poverty Action Group.

Peters, T (1989) *Thriving on chaos: handbook for a management revolution*, Pan.

Protherough, R (1989) In Wiegand, P and Raynor, M (eds), *Curriculum progress 5 to 16: school subjects and the National Curriculum debate*, Falmer Press, Chapter 5, 'English', 119–47.

Roehampton Institute (1994) *Juvenile reading habits*, BNBRF Report, The British Library.

Spears, L (ed) (1998) *Insights into leadership*, Wiley.

Wells, G (1982) *Language, learning and education*, Bristol University.

Whitehead, F et al (1977) *Children and their books*, Macmillan/Schools Council.

Working Party of the Literature Committee for the Scottish Arts Council (1989) *Readership report*, Scottish Arts Council.

# CHAPTER 1

# The context for children's library services

Peggy Heeks

> The public library is the only before and after form of learning support for reading . . . it is never too late in the library if you get chucked out of school. (Head of Library Service)

## Introduction

Nationally and internationally it has become commonplace to talk of the turbulent environment in which public services currently operate. A Place for Children research has shown the direct effects of such an environment on the managers and front-line staff who strive to maintain, and even improve, services, and on their clients. Following on from the issues identified in the introduction, this chapter looks at some of the key influences – from the global to the local – which affect children's librarianship today.

## The nature of current change

Change is a basic element of life, a necessary part of growth and development, as well as potentially destructive. As noted earlier, there are major changes facing all public sector services, with socio-economic factors being especially significant. Library services are responding variously to these changes, depending on local circumstances and needs.

## Demographic change

Child population figures vary widely in different parts of the country. So, while in our research Manchester reported a need to close schools, London forecast a rise in pupil numbers of 15% by 2003. In Birmingham, it was seen as crucial that segments of the child population were targeted according to need, with the youngest children being seen as especially deserving of resources:

> . . . number one is that we have a unique role in terms of the 0–3s.

Leeds had a similar priority:

> I think that we are the library service for the under fives . . .

but with the qualifying statement that:

> . . . the public library is the only before and after form of learning support for reading . . . It is never too late in the library if you get chucked out of school.

In Southwark there was also concentration on the under-fives and on the teenage years, and children with disabilities were another group for whom services were being developed. Targeting black children and those from ethnic minorities was also important, although population shifts had meant that in some inner-city areas the concept of 'ethnic minority' had changed:

> In most inner city schools they are far from being a minority, in fact it is white children who are in the minority . . . in time seeing black families per se as in need or needing our help is going to be ludicrous.

Whilst focusing on particular needs in the child population was important, one of the aims was also:

> . . . to ensure as many children as possible use the library . . . [and] join the library.

In Welsh-speaking authorities such as Ynys Môn, targeting of the primary age or even younger was a deliberate bias that arose from the 'missionary' aim of getting children hooked and using bilingual materials as early as possible.

There is clearly a danger in targeting too closely, though, where there is an overwhelming need for *all* the community to benefit from a library service. An estate in Northern Ireland South Eastern Education and Library Board's catchment area, in the highest area of unemployment in the UK, was in this category:

> You have only to look around to see the need of a library. This estate has been ravaged by the troubles, there is no home environment of books, there is low educational aspiration. There is no bookshop and no book buying tradition. (South Eastern Education and Library Board)

Rural library services had particular problems in dealing with the demographic diversity in their areas. Stirling served a population of only 82,000 over 850 square miles, with inevitable problems in spreading a service thinly across a wide area. Pre-school playgroups and teenagers were targeted, but again there was a need to recognize that all of the community needed books – children taking Asterix or Tintin into their homes had been found to benefit their parents' literacy skills too. In Sighthill Library in Edinburgh, the library was also clearly a family resource – a haven for the whole community in an area characterized by social problems. One five-year old pointed out his tenement flat through the library window:

*I can wave at my Mum from here.*

There was value in the socializing impact of a library serving the various demographic groups in its area, as well as targeting particular groups of young people. Edinburgh had taken this as its strategy with no specific targets for the service overall. There was equal distribution of resources across the age ranges, with needs targeted according to each community's circumstances.

The questionnaire survey showed some interesting variations in the ways that authorities rated the importance of serving the different age groups and categories of children, which will be explored further in Chapter 3. However, it is worth noting here that there was clear convergence on the importance of services for the pre-school years.

## Collaboration

Nationally, there have been calls for more collaboration between organizations supporting social and economic regeneration in communities. This is already having an impact on library services and is likely to become an increasingly important factor in cross-sectoral initiatives. At the local level, Birmingham and Manchester are among authorities mounting cross-departmental initiatives, but there are many factors which currently inhibit such cooperation. A number of the case studies confirmed Alan Dyson's observation that funding uncertainties create an unfavourable climate for joint work:

> The obsession in recent years with devolved management, the creation of internal markets and the setting of increasingly demanding targets within increasingly constrained budgets has made it almost impossible for these agencies to collaborate in order to address fundamental social problems. (Dyson, 1997, 9)

While partnerships between education, health and social service agencies may, as yet, be underdeveloped, partnership in general is a theme much in vogue. For example, the role of parents as partners in education is receiving unprecedented attention. It has moved from one of support to one of active participation, underpinned by home–school contracts. The subject was among those addressed by David Cracknell in his 1997 inaugural speech as President of the Society of Education Officers, when he promoted the notion of 'the learning family'. In the area of public/commercial sector relations there has also been a shift from schemes of sponsorship to those jointly organized, managed and financed. It is significant that the running of groups of schools in education action zones is open to private companies, and Croydon Borough has already joined with business to mount a bid with radical elements designed to provide a skills-based curriculum tailored more directly to the needs of employers. There have been claims that the opening of such opportunities to commercial companies amounts to a back-door privatization of education. It seems clear that in future the divide between public and private services will be far less clear-cut. Experience within the health sector confirms this. There is also a third force to be remembered: the 350,000 non-profit organizations in the UK. There is scope for a richer variety of partnerships involving this sector, business and central or local government.

The questionnaire survey showed that library services were indeed taking advantage of funding from the private sector, with 61% of the counties receiving funding support from local businesses, although much more could be done in this respect, with only 19% of authorities in Wales, 25% in Northern Ireland and 31% in London receiving private-sector funding. Generally, the percentage of authorities receiving external funding from all sources could be improved – EU funding had been received by only 8.7% of authorities, all of these county authorities.

## The National Literacy Project and the National Year of Reading

The need for more reliance on collaboration is illustrated by the major literacy initiatives now under way, which include the National Literacy Project and the National Year of Reading. W H Smith, for example, is providing £1.5 million for books from a list drawn up by the Department for Education and Employment (DFEE) to 400 schools selected by the department, in a scheme described by the Education and Employment Secretary as 'an excellent example of how this government and business can work together'. The UK Government has announced literacy targets to ensure that by 2002 80% of 11-year-olds in England and Wales reach Level 4 of the National Curriculum in English. As part of the drive for improvement, £4 million has been allocated to family literacy schemes, and parents are being asked to read to their children for 20 minutes a day. The importance of partnerships has been emphasized by Neil McClelland, director of The National Literacy Trust, who sees the development of literacy as requiring attention to two interdependent dimensions: the work of professional educators in schools, and 'the energies, imagination and skills' of the whole community. He cites the ten-year programme which has begun in Newcastle upon Tyne as a model which is gaining support in other authorities (McClelland, 1997, xvi).

Projects of this kind have the potential to bring together adults and children, public and business agencies, in responding to the challenge of making the UK a more literate country.

Collaborative initiatives with education and other services were regarded as important in the libraries we studied, but there needed to be an even greater effort to integrate collaboration more fully into service provision. Positive examples were Hampshire, where the School Library Service was about to take part in the 'Reading is fundamental' (RIFUK) initiative which was just beginning, and Croydon, where there had been a joint conference with the Education Department in response to *Investing in children* and primary schools were visited before the annual 'Book trail' promotion. In Birmingham the Bookstart pack was being provided to every baby who had a hearing check in the city (estimated at 10,000 in the first year alone). In Leeds, partnership was not only with education but also with the council as a whole, through its literacy development scheme. There were problems for new unitary authorities, however, in establishing themselves in new corporate structures. Partnerships outside the authority were sometimes easier to establish, such as the links between Ceredigion and the Welsh Books Council. A quiz for Welsh children was planned by the Council but administered by the county library service. Conversely, Edinburgh had very fully developed links across the authority, partly as a result of the head of service's well-established role in corporate management. She headed the council's Public Information Team and had a number of other cross-departmental responsibilities. A joint document had been produced with the education authority and there were plans to move forward to even more cooperative working.

## Information and communications technology (ICT)

Underpinning much of the move towards collaborative working is the increased opportunity for networking by means of technology. No country in the world is untouched by the developments in information and communications technology which have taken place over the past decade. In this country we have seen a major shift from an industrial age to a technological one, and already we can note both the benefits ensuing and the adjustments being made to work patterns and everyday life. The technology continues to evolve and we realize there are possibilities still unexplored, but the direction is clear. The global dimension of information technology has been grasped quickly in areas such as banking, commerce and journalism. However, several European countries have also understood the need to establish a national information policy, and the British government is being pressed to do the same. Within the UK, there is a drive to exploit our assets as an information-rich nation. The autumn of 1997 saw the publication of *Connecting the learning society* (Department for Education and Employment, 1997), which set out the government strategy behind the establishment of a 'grid for learning'. It is expected that by 2002 all schools, colleges, universities and libraries will be connected to a purpose-built Internet service. January 1998 saw the launch of a prototype website. The report *Preparing for the information age* showed the progress made on the UK's Superhighways Initiative since 1995 (Department for Education and Employment et al, 1997). Development is seen to involve not just provision of appropriate systems but extensive training programmes to develop skills in using them and awareness of their potential. In the new network society, people who are unconnected are increasingly at a disadvantage, and a new class, 'the information poor', is in danger of emerging. There is, therefore, a focus on improving service costs and patterns of accessibility. The development of Internet access was beginning to feature in all libraries studied – providing sufficient access for young people in libraries where even book funds were limited was, however, a considerable problem.

## Measures of success

We shall be examining the assessment of children's library services in detail in Chapter 6, but it is important to note here the widespread influence of the value for money, compulsory competitive tendering and now best value initiatives in local government in the UK. The previous Conservative administration placed an emphasis on value for money and accountability which had far-reaching effects on the culture of public services. Among that government's initiatives, the establishment of the charter mark scheme provided a way of bench-marking the quality of public services and raising standards. Similar aims are behind the extensive testing of pupils, the publication of league tables showing examination results and the programme of school inspections by OFST-ED (the Office for Standards in Education) in England and Wales. Precise measures of success have been drawn up for the national literacy campaign, as noted above.

Not only are there overall targets, but also local ones. A tightly structured literacy hour has been designed for primary schools, and has received a mixed reception from teachers and specialists. McClelland is among those emphasizing the complexity of the issues surrounding literacy and has warned of the dangers of methods aimed at short-term success rather than sustainable improvement. It has been felt necessary to make it clear that 'there are no quick fixes, no pedagogic panacea, no sound bite solutions to help build a literate nation.' (McClelland, 1997, xvi) The cross-currents within education are a symptom of uncertainty in the wider environment, and of political tendencies to over-simplify complex issues. Researchers from London University Institute of Education, commenting on the literacy targets, concluded: 'The problem with which the White Paper has to engage is that there exists no authentic way of measuring what is happening in the way that is being inadvertently suggested.' (Hackett, 1997, 3) Similarly, a key finding of research into school effectiveness shows that schools are not uniformly 'effective' or 'ineffective', but differentially so for different groups of children (Goldstein, 1997, 15).

Questions are being asked as to the effectiveness of the culture of inspection which has grown up. A 1997 survey carried out by the London School of Economics under the leadership of Professor Christopher Hood noted that in the past two decades expenditure on regulations had doubled to reach £1 billion a year, with apparently little consideration being given to the benefits and cost-effectiveness. For example, the cost of an OFSTED secondary school inspection is over £20,000 (Walker, 1997, 19). Doubts are also being voiced about the validity of applying a business model to public sector initiatives. The debate is less about the need for accountability than the way services can be assessed. Of the situation in North America, Childers and Van House observed: 'Society is concerned with return on its investment in services. There are strong pressures for accountability.' (Childers and Van House, 1993, 6)

## Local and central government

Over the past two decades there have been major shifts in the relationship between local and central government, with the 1988 Education Reform Act being a particularly significant agent of change. Some finances previously allocated to LEAs (local education authorities) were delegated to schools; some powers previously exercised by LEAs passed to the Secretary of State for Education. The role of local inspectors has diminished with the establishment of a national inspection system of considerable rigour in England and Wales. Both the 1988 Education and Housing Acts opened the way to the opting out of local government control. The introduction of compulsory competitive tendering further reduced local government's role as provider. Overall there has been a significant attenuation of local government power. While there are many signs of alienation between local and central government during the period 1988 to 1997, the situation under the Labour administration, elected in May 1997, is less clear.

The new literacy standards offer an example. The targets have been set by the DFEE but the local authorities will be made accountable for ensuring that they are met. Partnerships between schools and LEAs may be strengthened by the education development plans which every local authority must put in place by 1999. Authorities will have to negotiate Key Stage 2 and GCSE (General Certificate of Secondary Education) targets for every maintained school and explain how they will be met. Final control, however, rests with the centre, for plans must be approved by the Education and Employment Secretary. The Schools Standards and Framework Bill, currently working its way through Parliament, sets out new duties for local authorities, establishes a code of practice to define responsibilities, and increases the Secretary of State's powers to intervene.

Further scrutiny of LEAs will come through the inspections planned by both OFSTED and the Audit Commission. The context is given in a report by the Commission, *Changing partners*, which shows that fundamental questions – for example, on roles and ways of measuring performance – have still to be addressed (Audit Commission, 1998). Many of the tensions between local and central government spring from the complexity of funding arrangements. At a time of rising council taxes set against cuts in service, it is easy for each side to blame the other. There are frequently accusations that central government is favouring local authorities of its own political persuasion, while central government condemns waste or poor financial management at local levels. The council tax increases for 1998–9 average 5.5% in London, 7.2% in other metropolitan areas, but 11.8% in shire counties, and there have been subsequent complaints that the revised formula for calculating government grants has reduced allocations to shire counties in respect of social services, pre-school children and capital schemes. The largest part of local authority budgets is spent on education, with only a minor share of the total raised locally by the council tax. There has recently been concern that funds allocated by central government for school purposes may be diverted by local councillors for other services, and that local authorities retain too much of the education budget for administrative purposes. At present the standard spending assessment (SSA) forms the basis of each council's budget, but it has been the subject of controversy ever since its introduction in 1990. In 1998 nearly 100 authorities sent delegations to Whitehall to protest about their allocation. There are pressures for a move towards direct funding of education from Whitehall, yet in some ways the present ambivalence may suit both sides.

Such tensions provide the background for the substantial change currently in progress. In April 1997, 13 new authorities were established in England, and a further 18 in April 1998. Taking some earlier changes into account, 45 new LEAs are being created in England, with change on an even greater scale in Scotland and Wales. It is too early to assess the results of this reorganization: increased costs, the loss of specialist services and the demoralization of staff have to be set against the greater responsiveness which small-scale authorities encourage. Overall, the tensions within local government reflect the uncertainty of the environment in which public services are currently operating, with the establishment of a regional tier of government creating yet more potential for change.

## Public librarianship: the external environment

All the factors noted in the earlier sections of this chapter affect public librarianship, and make the work of managing services more challenging. The volatility of the environment makes strategic planning extremely difficult. For example, Hampshire Library Service had a £1-million cut in book fund imposed by a coalition council – a move opposed by Conservative members, who made its restoration a major issue in their 1997 election campaign, and were subsequently successful. In Northern Ireland, the Department of Education for Northern Ireland (DENI) required substantial budget cuts from the Education and Library Boards for 1997/98 and took the unprecedented step of announcing that the reductions should come from public library book funds. Book budgets were therefore, without warning, cut by about 50%.

## Local government reorganization

Other change imposed from outside has come from the local government reorganization mentioned above. The creation of smaller units has brought an increase in departments or directorates spanning a range of functions – for example, leisure, cultural or community services. In these cases the library section may have to work hard to maintain a high profile; on the credit side, such amalgamations open the way to new collaborative initiatives of the kind noted above. We found evidence of both the advantages and the disadvantages of the reorganization in the case studies. One chief librarian reported fresh energy coming from the change, with an impetus to redefine objectives and opportunities to work in an interdisciplinary way. Another authority had suffered such a reduction in professional staff that specialist services were suffering. Attempts to work in cooperation with neighbouring authorities were failing because of different approaches and priorities. The 1995–7 budget survey from the Library and Information Statistics Unit (LISU) found great diversity in funding levels and concluded that 'the mould of high and low spending authorities seems firmly set.' (Hanratty and Sumsion, 1996, 9) Views gathered during our study suggested that local government reorganization will increase variability in standards.

## Current standards of provision

Public library statistics reveal a range of problems. In the period 1984/85 to 1994/95, immediately prior to the start of our study, expenditure in the UK fell by 12% and loans by 19%, mainly in the area of adult fiction. Equally significant are movements within budgets, where the proportion spent on materials has decreased to 14%, while that on staff has increased to 53% although the number of staff has gone down (Sumsion, Creaser and Hanratty, 1996). This is clearly a perturbing situation for a service set up to give the public access to a wide range of books. There are doubts whether some library authorities are able to provide 'a comprehensive service' as required by the 1964 UK Public Libraries and Museums Act. A 1996 survey found that 'These statistics show a continued unfavourable trend in the offer to the library user.' (Hanratty and Sumsion, 1996, 8)

It may seem strange that, against this background, the past few years have seen a focus on quality of service. It is, perhaps, an illustration of the complexity of the current environment that we can have, simultaneously, declining standards and a search for quality. The period of national standards in public librarianship has probably gone. It is unlikely that we shall see a revision of the 1962 standards (Bourdillon, 1962) in the next few years. The move is rather towards local charters, on the line of the Library Association's 1993 model (Library Association, 1993). The difference between objective national standards and local charters is significant, for the latter promise to show a new closeness to the customer. The wish, indeed imperative, to strengthen the client base is shown also in the surveys of users and non-users, which are now an important source of management information. Examples of such surveys were provided by questionnaire respondents, although more needs to be done. Surveys of teenagers' reading were particularly mentioned – 16 projects were identified. The CIPFA Plus survey is also being taken up by authorities (see Chapter 3).

## Partnerships

Partnerships are still relatively underdeveloped in British public librarianship as we noted above. Income generation comes mainly from the library's own resources, particularly loans of audiovisual materials. Sponsorship applies mainly to promotional activities. Partnerships with book trade agencies have suffered a setback with the abolition of the Net Book Agreement, which has reduced profit margins for library suppliers and had a subsequent effect on joint initiatives. While schools are making increasing use of volunteers, their use in public libraries is very small. As has already been noted, energy which might have gone into designing partnership schemes is being spent on ensuring survival. Even when the library department is part of a wider directorate, the partnership principle does not seem to be sufficiently integrated into service provision.

## National public library reports

The various statistical surveys from Loughborough University's Library and Information Statistics Unit (LISU) are extremely valuable in providing a regular source of information and help in discerning trends. Supplementing these from 1993 to 1997 have been five major reports on the British public library service.

## Comedia

First came Comedia's examination of public library role and purpose *Borrowed time?*, which perceived a policy vacuum, nationally and locally, that was contributing to a marginalization of libraries. A clearer rationale, capable of articulation to the whole range of funders and clients, was urgent (Comedia, 1993). *Borrowed time?* was realistic about the environment within which public libraries will have to operate:

> Whilst the book will not disappear and will remain popular in all kinds of ways, its relative position in relation to other media will change. The book, in fact, is in many cases an inferior and cumbersome tool for finding what you want . . . Media literacy and computer literacy are now increasingly seen as necessary in a world in which people are bombarded with images and information largely on air and on screen – throughout their waking hours. The ability to interpret, judge and understand the processes and meaning of the media environ-

ment is seen as essential. The ability to log on and operate computers . . . is today possibly as important as the ability to write with paper and pen. (Comedia, 1993)

## Aslib Review

Aslib's *Review of the public library service in England and Wales* (Aslib, 1995) came next, described as the largest piece of research into public libraries ever undertaken in the world. To a large extent it was a scoping study. It identified new factors as information technology, partnerships with other libraries, and collaborative enterprises bringing in private and voluntary factors. Cooperation was a major theme of the report. The dilemma of public libraries, caught between lobbying against cuts and promoting a positive image, was clearly understood, and the advice to managers was to 'find ways to break the shackles of today's problems', to enable them to address the critical issues of tomorrow.

The year 1997 saw the publication of three national reports with a number of common themes.

## Reading the future

*Reading the future*, from the Department of National Heritage, was the Government's belated response to the Aslib *Review* and *Investing in Children*. It suggested that public libraries had, over the years, shifted away from their original 'high seriousness' towards entertainment, and identified information technology as a means of restoring 'the profound importance of public libraries in our society.' (Department of National Heritage, 1997, 3) Long overdue, the report received a mixed reception in the professional press and probably came too close to a general election to make a great impact (Black and Muddiman, 1997; Usherwood, 1997).

## Due for renewal

The Audit Commission's report on the library service *Due for renewal* (Audit Commission, 1997) confirmed the problems arising from reductions in opening hours, decline in issues and rising staff costs, and offered a number of practical suggestions. The recommendations focused on forging partnerships, making greater use of information and communications technology, and improving three key aspects of management: overall planning, stock management and service costing.

## New library: the people's network

The Library and Information Commission was established in 1995 to be a focus of expertise and a source of advice to the Government. Among its interests is production of a research strategy, and already it is apparent that a fundamental theme in its work is the impact and value of library and information services. The link between research and practice will be accorded greater importance. It was a working group of the Commission which produced the report *New library: the people's network*. This argued that public libraries are the ideal vehicle for providing access to new information channels, and held that 'a transformation of libraries' must take place, re-equipping them and reskilling their staff. 'Enhancing education and lifelong learning opportunities for children and adults' was listed first among priorities (Library and Information Commission, 1997, ii).

## Connecting the learning society

A report from the DFEE, *Connecting the learning society*, sets out a number of options for establishing a National Grid for Learning to connect every school in Britain to the information superhighway, with schools connecting to each other and linking to all learning institutions, whether libraries, colleges, universities, museums or galleries. It also emphasizes the place of public libraries in this development (Department for Education and Employment, 1997).

Both reports therefore complement and reinforce the argument for a national network.

## Vision

In a rapidly changing environment, the sense of direction and confidence which vision gives has become even more necessary. A major task for managers is finding a vision which incorporates the challenges identified in recent national reports as well as giving due weight to the traditional services which generate much public goodwill. It should be far from a lone task. The project case studies show the importance managers place on building a shared vision. One authority, for example, puts each year's plan out for consultation, and arranges staff seminars for discussion of priorities, options and resource implications. National reports and Library Association guidelines may be helpful, but essentially building the vision has to be a locally generated task and responsive to the local community. The process may, in fact probably will, result in slimming down the library's work programme. Among the case studies, one head of department commented: '*We are going to have to differentiate more clearly between an education and a leisure role.*' Another had established three key service directions: information service, work with children and young people, and reader development. There is some similarity here with Oxfordshire's new focus on the reader, and with moves elsewhere from a stock-focused strategy to a reader-focused strategy. A revival of interest in readers' advisory services has been identified in a study by Kinnell and Shepherd (1998);

and a staff role as enabler and facilitator, information consultant and educator, involving 'a cultural shift' forms part of the agenda of *New library* (Library and Information Commission, 1997, iii).

Whatever priorities are determined, it is obviously important that they reflect the local authority's strategic plan, and we found several examples of such a close association. The project interviews brought evidence of both the energy which can be generated by a shared vision and the deterioration which can set in without it:

*The government has identified a gap in provision, and it's up to us to be in there.*

*There is a general malaise here. It's part of a vicious spiral where long-term financial starvation breeds staff depression and lack of enthusiasm, leading to a dearth of fresh ideas.*

The need for vision is urgent, but comments from another area show the context in which some libraries are trying to formulate it:

*We need a vision from the top. Our objectives need spelling out. We've spent so much time fighting to survive that we're in danger of forgetting why libraries were set up.*

## Children's librarianship

Children's library services can be regarded as among the most successful aspects of current public librarianship. With issues exceeding 111 million annually and representing a growing percentage of the whole, it is an area receiving increasing attention nationally and locally. However, while many aspects of the external environment offer opportunities for children's librarianship, it too suffers from the unpredictability of the climate within which public services currently operate.

## Social factors

The appropriateness of the title 'A Place for Children' on which this book is based was confirmed by the case studies. Awareness of physical needs was apparent in ramps for buggies, toilets and baby-changing facilities. Great effort had been taken to make even the smallest children's sections attractive and welcoming: among larger libraries Birmingham, Croydon and Southampton were outstanding. The questionnaire responses show libraries giving high priority to pre-school children, partly because it is at this stage that attitudes to books are formed. The importance being accorded to parents in educational circles is reflected in children's librarianship. It is part of the focus generally on customers and stakeholders. Parents' collections are the norm in larger libraries and parents are drawn into the activities programme:

*We have friendly, approachable staff who make time for children and their parents, and we model adult–children sharing to make parents aware of the value of books.*

The social value of libraries was currently the subject of research at Sheffield University (Linley and Usherwood, 1998) and that aspect will be explored further in Chapter 6. It is sufficient to record here that the research provided plenty of evidence of the importance of library visits to children's social development. This applied throughout the age groups, from young children's first encounters with a community building, through class visits of primary school children, to teenage use as a drop-in centre.

## Educational factors

The effect of the National Curriculum was apparent in the stock of non-fiction which children's libraries had built up to meet demand – the Romans, the Vikings, the Victorians etc. In some cases reference collections on some subjects had been set aside to ensure that at least some information was always available. Reductions in school library services, or the opting out of subscription schemes, are also putting increased pressure on public library stocks. The various literacy initiatives highlight the importance of books and are therefore of potential importance to children's librarians. In some education circles there is fear that requirements such as the literacy hour will do little more than generate 'a new culture of targets' (Hackett, 1997) and librarians were at pains to present a different perspective:

*There is a whole agenda around literacy in education which is too narrowly defined. We have a role in broadening perceptions of what reading and imagination are about.*

*Libraries have a big role in helping children develop the higher reading skills of scanning, skimming, selecting what's relevant.*

There are several signs that the connection between children's librarianship and education is inadequate. For example, only 39% of questionnaire respondents rated support for formal education as 'very important'. The study found response to education issues such as under-achievement of boys or growth of summer schools patchy. Similarly, the public library seems to be invisible to some educationists. For example, an OFSTED report on primary school children in inner London noted: 'They may well not experience much, if any, support at home; they are unlikely to have access to a rich stock of literature.' (Blatchford, 1997) There is no recognition here of the help a local library might give. Even where lip-service is paid by politicians to the importance of public libraries in the encouragement of reading, rarely is this translated into including libraries in national reading initiatives.

## Financial factors

The uncertain financial climate affecting public librarianship generally has, expectedly, repercussions on services to children. The 1997 statistics from LISU, figures for the point at which our data were being gathered, show a decline in funds for materials from 1991–2 to 1997–8, dropping from £1.49 to £1.39 per capita, with a consequent effect on stock levels (Creaser and Murphy, 1997). Perhaps even more perturbing than the overall figures are the strong fluctuations within the countries of the United Kingdom which these averages hide. The sudden budget cuts in Northern Ireland are a particularly distressing example of change imposed from outside. In one board area, for example, a 1996 materials budget of £120,000 was reduced in 1997 to £26,000, to provide for a library membership of 52,000 children served through 26 branches. Reductions in core funding have made competition for project funds more intense, but there were reservations about the climate generated by such opportunities:

*Is the work being skewed to obtain project funds? There are so many projects that there is no time to reflect on their results or learn from them.*

Even in the present difficult financial climate, most authorities (83%) reported development areas. These reflected the themes running through the case studies: services to pre-school children and teenagers, literacy support and information technology facilities. A sign of current uncertainty, though, can be seen in the small amount of in-house research reported, undertaken by less than a quarter of respondents. Change is also occurring in the relationship between children's libraries and book suppliers, through the end of the Net Book Agreement. When a standard price for all titles applied, suppliers competed with one another through services and discounts. Now profit margins have been reduced, less money is available to support library promotions, and the continuing viability of approval collections is in doubt.

## Staffing factors

Given that the proportion of library budgets spent on staffing is increasing, it behoves authorities to ensure that expenditure under this heading is justified in terms of value for money. In the majority of case studies services to children were directed by specialists rather than generalist staff, and this approach was seen as essential to success:

*A generalist approach cuts staff off from specialist knowledge of books and clients. Our structures enable children's work to flourish.*

*We have the largest number of children's librarians of any authority. It is essential to have specialist librarians who are well-read, can guide children from one book to another, match and extend inter-est. That is the way children's reading develops.*

Staff attitudes and a bedrock of book knowledge were repeatedly cited as major elements in successful service. Yet the same cross-currents are apparent in children's librarianship as in public librarianship generally, and in the wider environment. Set against staffing patterns in the case studies is the questionnaire finding that 37% of authorities have no specialist children's team. Nor have the role and training of para-professionals been clearly established. For example, in one authority they help run holiday activities and take part in meetings of specialists. In another they feel cut off from the clients:

*Libraries should be a community resource, but the children's library here seems very separate. As for training about children's work, para-professionals are not really considered for that.*

## Conclusions

Within children's librarianship there are seemingly opposed trends: one towards self-service, helped by stock categorization; the other towards services that are intensive and client-focused. Is children's librarianship old-fashioned, or does it point the way to the development of a whole range of specialist services in which the librarian serves as advisor? The 1997 LISU survey showed a reduction in the number of professional library staff engaged in work with children. It now stands at 624 for the whole of the United Kingdom, approximately one per 17,000 children. This figure seems appallingly low, especially when set against the potential part public libraries could play in raising standards of literacy.

It is a measure of the importance now given to children's library services that many of the national reports already referred to draw attention to their value. For example, the authors of Aslib's *Review* read current trends as suggesting 'that the need for children's services will increase in the future.' (Aslib, 1995, 54) The Library and Information Commission's *2020 vision* statement, while urging a holistic rather than sectoral approach, drew attention to the value of providing resources for 'particular user groups, especially children and young people.' (Library and Information Commission, 1996) *Investing in children* produced many specific recommendations, some of which have already been followed up by research or specific initiatives (Library and Information Services Council, 1995). The 1997 revision of the Library Association guidelines for services to children and young people took note of issues raised in *Investing in children*, and has been welcomed as offering a frame of reference for local work (Blanshard, 1997). Evidence from the case studies shows both to have had an influence on practice.

## References

Aslib (1995) *Review of the public library service in England and Wales for the Department of National Heritage*, Aslib.

Audit Commission (1997) *Due for renewal: a report on the library service*, Audit Commission.

Audit Commission (1998) *Changing partners*, Audit Commission.

Black, A and Muddiman, D (1997) Myths of a golden age, *Library Association Record*, **99** (5), 256.

Blanshard, C (ed), (1997) *Children and young people: Library Association guidelines for public library services*, 2nd edn, Library Association Publishing.

Blatchford, R (1997) 'Reading is fundamental' and the SLA unite for reading, *School Librarian*, **45** (1), 4–5.

Bourdillon, H (1962) *Standards of public library service in England and Wales*, HMSO.

Childers, T A and Van House, N A (1993) *What's good: describing your public library's effectiveness*, American Library Association.

Comedia (1993) *Borrowed time?: the future of public libraries in the United Kingdom*, Comedia.

Creaser, C and Murphy, A (1997) *A survey of library services to schools and children in the UK, 1996–97*, Loughborough University Library and Information Statistics Unit.

Department for Education and Employment (1997) *Connecting the learning society: a national grid for learning*, DFEE.

Department for Education and Employment et al (1997) *Preparing for the information age: synoptic report of the education department's superhighways initiative*, DFEE.

Department of National Heritage (1997) *Reading the future: a review of public libraries in England*, DNH.

Dyson, A (1997) Time to reconnect, *Times Educational Supplement*, (26 December).

Goldstein, H (1997) From raw to half-baked, *Times Educational Supplement*, (18 July).

Hackett, G (1997) Researchers' warning on national tests, *Times Educational Supplement*, (24 October).

Hanratty, C and Sumsion, J (1996) *Public library materials fund and budget survey 1995–97*, Loughborough University Library and Information Statistics Unit.

Kinnell, M and Shepherd, J (1998) *Adult reading promotion in UK public libraries*, Taylor-Graham.

Library and Information Commission (1996) *2020 vision*, LIC.

Library and Information Commission Working Group on Information Technology (1997) *New library: the people's network*, LIC.

Library and Information Services Council (England) Working Party on Library Services for Children and Young People (1995) *Investing in children: the future of library services for children and young people*, Library Information Series 22, HMSO.

Library Association (1993) *A charter for public libraries*, Library Association.

Linley, R and Usherwood, R (1998) *New measures for the new library: a social audit of pub-*

*lic libraries*, British Library Research and Innovation Centre Report 89, University of Sheffield Centre for the Public Library in the Information Society.

McClelland, N (ed) (1997) *Building a literate nation: the strategic agenda for literacy over the next five years*, Trentham Books.

Sumsion, J, Creaser, C and Hanratty, C (1996) *LISU annual library statistics 1996*, Loughborough University Library and Information Statistics Unit.

Usherwood, R (1997) I have read the future and ... , *Library Association Record*, **99** (4), 96–7.

Walker, D (1997) Army of regulators cost taxpayers £1 billion, *Times Educational Supplement*, (17 October).

# CHAPTER 2

# The role of the children's library in supporting literacy

Ray Lonsdale

Public libraries are the driving force for children's reading from
the earliest ages (Croydon)

## Introduction

Traditionally, a central tenet of the British public library service to children has been
the importance of supporting reading and literacy. This is embodied in the various
statements which have been issued on the aims and objectives for children's libraries
in the UK. In the late 1970s the Public Library Research Group (PLRG) set out its
consideration of the primary objectives, amongst which were:

> To promote and encourage reading as a means of self development and to encourage an
> awareness of the pleasure of reading . . .

> To assist language development and improve reading standards . . . (Brown, 1979, 382).

Just over ten years later the influential Library Association guidelines, *Children and young
people*, reaffirmed the importance of the public library in facilitating the development of
language acquisition, in particular the acquisition of vocabulary, speech and language
skills, and the acquisition of reading skills (Library Association, 1991, 8–9). The second edition of that work, published in 1997, echoed these aims (Blanshard, 1997).

There can be no doubting that children's libraries have a long-established remit to
support literacy. However, these statements offer only broad conceptions of reading
and literacy. There has been little in the professional literature to indicate how libraries
might define 'literacy' or what types of literacy they actively support. Our research set
out to address these issues.

## Role of the public library in supporting reading literacy

There was uniform agreement amongst library authorities that they have a central responsibility to support reading literacy. The results of the questionnaire survey reflect this, although a surprising 5% of respondents saw it as less than essential. Most case study authorities revealed an almost messianic zeal in their belief about their role in promoting reading literacy as exemplified in the following statement:

> *Public libraries are the driving force for children's reading development from the earliest ages. The Bookstart projects have demonstrated that. We forge partnerships with parents. No other institution is able to do that. Experience in this building shows that if you provide a quality service, people will flock to it.* (Croydon)

Some authorities indicated that there were times in the child's development when the public library's contribution to supporting reading is particularly critical. In citing the Bookstart initiatives which have been growing throughout the UK, the previous quotation reflects the singular importance of early literacy, developing rapport with the parents and carers and the pre-school child. The head of library services in Birmingham echoes this sentiment in the following statement:

> *I do see it as absolutely crucial. I think number one is that we have a unique role in terms of the 0–3s. We know from all the research that is when the crucial interventions tend to happen. The library is an enormously important resource for parents . . . they have the courage and the background knowledge of what they can achieve simply by reading, talking and listening with their children . . . The early literacy, pre-reading skills I see as absolutely crucial. We have always given them a lot of priority in the allocation of resources and energy. If we ever had to cut back I felt determined this wasn't an area where we would cut back.*

The perceptions librarians hold about the significance of the pre-school child is matched by the emphasis which is placed on this group when we sought their responses on actual provision of services (see Chapter 4). Our studies sought to probe further how children's libraries perceive reading literacy. A number of dimensions of reading support were identified (see Figure 2.1).

## Reading skills acquisition

There is an ambivalence amongst authorities as to their role in formally supporting the reading process, i.e. having a remit to inculcate specific reading skills. Fewer authorities saw this as a major aim (Figure 2.1), although some of those who advocated this were adamant that they had a remit to attend to reading skills acquisition – arising possibly from the specific circumstances associated with their education authority:

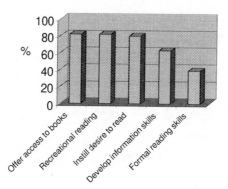

**Fig. 2.1** *Importance of types of reading support*

*The role of the library has become more important as reading skills have suffered because of the time taken up by the Northern Ireland curriculum. We are increasingly filling the gap. Libraries have also a big role in helping primary and pre-school children develop the higher reading skills of scanning, skimming, selecting what's relevant.* (South Eastern Education and Library Board)

Few librarians verbalized such support in the case study interviews. However, another statistic gleaned from our questionnaire survey revealed that almost 90% did believe they had a central role to play in supporting information skills (Figure 2.1). No finer analysis on this issue was possible. One could postulate, however, that – as implied in the above quotation – reading skills such as skimming and scanning, amongst others, might be inculcated through information skills programmes. Although only 57% of authorities provided programmes (see Chapter 5), it may well be that a higher degree of reading skills instruction is currently being undertaken.

In the main, however, our study revealed that the majority of authorities believed that the responsibility for reading skills acquisition lay firmly within the school:

*We have a subsidiary aim of supporting schoolwork. Reading has a value in children's personal, social and imaginative development. We work to promote the enjoyment of sharing books. Promotion of literacy is less important to us.* (Southampton)

For some libraries the roles of the school and the public library appear clearly differentiated:

*I see us as having quite a strong role, a primary role in actually helping children to learn how to read. Not in the formal, educational sense, but just in the sense of giving children that sensual knowledge background, a feel for the reality of the whole thing that I think is probably an essential prerequisite for children reading . . .*

*While we do not resource the classroom, and with good reason, schools should be the single most import-*

*ant access point to children. Working closely with schools, however, means that the role of the public library service needs to be clearly separated from that of the education library service to avoid a blurring of boundaries. Children know the difference between the two and they are aware of the context in which the two services stand.* (Southwark)

However, the need to establish a rapport between the two parties is evident in the rider:

*A lot more could, and should be done on a strategic level working alongside the education library service.* (Southwark)

Other library services already have in place mechanisms to reflect their clear cooperation:

*We're trying to build up a strategy of cooperation, and have just set up Telemeet, linking two branches and six schools to the Internet and CD-ROM network.* (Croydon)

## Developing a desire and love of reading

If public libraries accord a low priority to supporting formal reading skills development, what do they perceive as the promotion of reading literacy? Our study showed that great importance is placed upon fostering recreational reading and instilling the desire to read rather than on promoting the development of reading skills through the formal education of the child (see Figure 2.2).

This philosophy was manifest in many of the responses collected during the case studies:

*We show reading as being an enjoyable experience, in an environment not judged by grades. The library complements the schools' efforts on the teaching of reading, and it forwards school projects. It motivates children to read.* (North Eastern Education and Library Board)

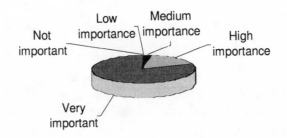

**Fig. 2.2** *Instilling a desire to read*

*Public libraries should support the work of the school, but as a leisure activity.* (Hampshire)

The inculcation of a love for books and an enjoyment of reading ranks high in the stated aims of authorities. This correlates with the guidance given in the major professional guidelines and seminal works on children's librarianship (Library Association, 1991; Elkin and Lonsdale, 1996; Blanshard, 1997):

> *I think library services are there to encourage children and parents to have a love of books, to have a love of literature and to want to read and to practise the reading skills. And so, given all of that, then the nature of what we are doing is part of a continuum, and in order to enjoy books and in order to benefit from books and in order to have literacy, you need to be able to read, and so one of the essential parts of what we do is to encourage children to read, to give them opportunities to read and through promotions and various activities to keep them reading.* (Northamptonshire)

> *Promoting and encouraging a love of reading, stimulating a desire to read more widely, demonstrating the pleasure that lies in reading.* (North Eastern Education and Library Board)

> *The enjoyment aspect and how it can enable children to grow. We do have a very important role in supporting literacy, partly through that enjoyment . . . We know very clearly that we come across children who are quite skilled at reading but really don't want to read. So part of our role is also to help encourage those children in whatever way we can by working with schools or working with children individually. It may have been painful learning to read or they perhaps haven't seen the wide range of material which is available and choose not to read.* (Birmingham)

> *Our policy objectives include 'To promote the enjoyment of reading'. A lot of effort is put into fulfilling that objective in the children's service, using a variety of approaches. A lot of what we have done has been ad hoc. The structures enable children's work to flourish. [In] the Year of Reading, 1998, . . . we [looked] at a strategic approach.* (Croydon)

Implicit in the last statement is a theme which we discovered running through many of our discussions with other library authorities. This is the desire to ensure that the collections and the promotional approaches which need to be established to fulfil the heuristic dimension of reading support should be part of a strategic plan and not simply ad hoc. This is an issue that receives further consideration in Chapter 5.

## Self-development and social awareness

The PLRG objectives referred to earlier suggest that reading is a means of self-development, and of extending and developing cultural awareness (Brown, 1979, 382). This sentiment is shared in both editions of *Children and young people* (Library Association, 1991; Blanshard, 1997). In *Children and young people* one of the major purposes of reading is to facilitate self-knowledge, identity (both individual and cultural), a knowledge of the wider world and a greater understanding of other people, cultures and situations – perceptions which are also embodied in the seminal report *Investing in children* (LISC(E), 1995).

The public libraries which we surveyed concurred with the pronouncements in the professional literature. There are two dimensions to this, the first concerns the act of reading *per se*.

> It [reading] has a distinct role. Reading develops social awareness, and the library provides children with a rare opportunity to choose for themselves, and opportunity for self-expression and discrimination. They have a unique degree of freedom to do what they want. Library staff are not trying to sell them anything, so the relationship with them is special. (Southampton)

> Children's emergent literacy is only a part of the issue, though. There is a lot more than that. Libraries are the only service a child can join and use independently. Literacy needs to be defined in broad terms, and the social development of children is tied in with that. The educationalist Wygotski holds that children learn through social processes. (Northamptonshire)

> To encourage a belief in the value and enjoyment of reading among children and the adults who care for, and work with them. The stock selected must support this objective by actively encouraging all children to enjoy books and reading. It is also important for the service to recognise that every child has a relatively unknown potential for personal development. It is therefore our particular responsibility to ensure that all children have the opportunity to find their own level and to explore and choose from collections representing the whole range of children's literature. (Essex – Stock Selection Policy: Children and Schools)

Others perceive the importance of socialization as a consequence of the various activities associated with reading:

> There's also the importance of social development in a public environment, of moving around with confidence, of being part of a group in sharing stories. (Croydon)

> The library visits widen their social experiences, as the children engage with a different environment, different people. They're made to feel that the library is a place for them, not just for adults. Everyone feels at home, but they also learn they have responsibilities in their behaviour and care of books. On the one hand it's an agreeable place to come to with friends; on the other it's a stimulating place where they have to concentrate as they search for information, or stretch their minds through new reading choices. (North Eastern Education and Library Board)

Margaret Jackson (1993) and Margaret Meek (1991), amongst other observers, stress that literacy should not be synonymous with reading skills acquisition, but emphasize the importance of developing critical and evaluative skills, and of children applying reading to their social and cultural context. Literacy becomes, therefore, a critical agent in the process of empowerment.

> Fully literate children have the potential to control themselves and their environment through access to information, ideas, opinions; such is the power of literacy that teaching it could be defined as 'empowerment'. (Jackson, 1993)

Whilst most writers from the field of literacy studies see the acquisition of such skills as being the primary responsibility of schools, the contribution that public libraries (and school libraries) make in supporting the inculcation of these skills through information skills programmes must not be overlooked. In this sense we can conjecture that children's librarians are contributing to that broader definition of literacy.

## Access to books

The responsibility which the library has to bring children to appropriate reading materials figured highly in our survey, with 82% of authorities rating it as highly important (see Figures 2.1 and 2.3). This statistic was borne out in the data that we collected from the case studies. In particular, several authorities commented on the lack of suitable reading materials, both within the schools sector and within the home. This was an issue that was raised by authorities which were not experiencing social deprivation.

## The new literacies

Literacy studies have placed increasing importance on the need to extend the definition to include the reading of electronic formats (Barton, 1994; Meek, 1991; McGarry, 1994; Willinsky, 1990; Wray et al, 1989). These, amongst a number of writers, suggest that 'literacy' should encompass not only reading and writing but also the new

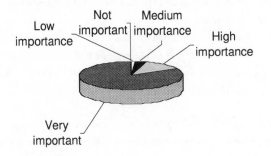

**Fig. 2.3** *Providing access to books*

literacies: a generic term used for other types of literacy – visual, graphic and computer-oriented. These writers acknowledge that the process of reading extends beyond
the printed word to encompass decoding of visual and non-linear forms. Recent
research into reading and hypertext suggest that there are unique skills associated with
the interpretation of language in hypertext, which is frequently portrayed in a non-linear form (Nielsen, 1997; Meyer, 1994). Studies have also revealed that reading on the
screen is 30% slower than from the printed page (Arjoon, 1999, 132). Another
important field of research has focused upon the differences between interactive CD-
ROMs and printed sources as regards access to and manipulation of data, and assim-
ilation of information (Large et al, 1994). The conclusions point to a need for
librarians to be cognisant of the different values accorded by children to audio, visual
and hypertext information.

How do public libraries perceive the importance of these forms of literacy? To what
extent do they support the inculcation of these skills amongst children? Interestingly,
the seminal guidelines to children's libraries (Blanshard, 1997) do not appear to extend
the notion of literacy. It appears to be synonymous with reading:

> The library service has a key role in fostering literacy . . . by providing and promoting mat-
> erial which assists reading development in young people . . .

> Literacy begins with language development, and language begins for young children through
> interaction with the caring adult. All of the library's *book* [my italics] stock is therefore rel-
> evant . . . (Blanshard, 1997, 21)

Earlier studies suggested that there was, at best, an ambivalence about the role of the
library in supporting new literacies, and at worst, hostility (Lonsdale and Wheatley,
1990; Denham, 1997). We also encountered such sentiments in our study:

> *Reading is seen as a print-based activity. Other kinds of literacy are not bothered with.*

Our investigations, however, suggested that an interesting change in attitude was occurring. Eighty per cent of authorities perceived non-book literacy (non-linear reading as
found in hypertext and multimedia, for example) as being of significance; indeed this
approached reading literacy in terms of its significance. The following statements are
typical of a number of authorities that indicated their belief in extending the traditional concept of reading literacy:

> *Libraries have also a big role in helping primary and pre-school children develop the higher reading
> skills of scanning, skimming, selecting what's relevant, which are needed to use new technology fruit-
> fully. We should be working even harder on these. At present the technology is ahead of the child. They
> trust what comes out of a machine too much. Faced with a CD-ROM or an encyclopaedia in print*

*form, children choose the CD, but their understanding is poor.* [This echoes Large's findings (Large et al, 1994).] *Too often the approach is 'copy, cut, paste'. Children should be asking, 'Is there another source?'; 'Why is that?'. Who will encourage this if not the librarian?* (South Eastern Education and Library Board)

*IT in relation to our role in reading is interesting. The use of CD-ROMs. I don't know if using a story on CD-ROM encourages children to read the printed version. If there is text on the screen perhaps it enhances what they do in terms of their reading? I think there is certainly a sharing there. You see a parent with a very young child sharing that experience of using a story based CD-ROM. The Stories from the Web project will be interesting in terms of that interaction around the story.* (Birmingham)

However, further investigation revealed that, while these attitudes were genuinely held by library staff, they were not necessarily manifest in the degree to which the library services and collections reflected the view. Only just over half of authorities believed that their collections and services reinforced the importance of non-book literacies.

We sought to divide the new literacies into two further groups: *graphic literacy*, which encompasses books with illustrations, graphic novels and comics; and *visual literacy* comprising non-book materials such as posters and advertisements. There is an increasing body of evidence that demonstrates the singular contribution that comics, amongst the various graphic forms, can make to improving reading development and promoting the reading habit. Contrary to the mythology that has accused comics of having an adverse effect on their readers, several studies have revealed that comic reading actually improves literacy:

A hell of a lot more adults read comics than are prepared to admit [it] in public; but you will be hard put to it to find any who *only* read comics. You *will* find many who never read anything at all except maybe the football results because they never learned to do it for pleasure. (Glancy, 1982, 11)

Children who read comics avidly also tended to read books avidly and vice versa. (Moon, 1977, 27)

It is gratifying, therefore, to discover that more status was given to graphic and visual literacies which not only support the child in interpreting illustrative data in books, but also contribute directly to their reading development:

As well as doing education-related things like vocabulary, reading ability, there is also children's experience of art. The large picture books we have will also form the children's judgement of how pictures can be drawn and depicted in a variety of styles. (Leeds)

As we shall see later, it is evident from the survey that more library authorities recognize the importance of ensuring that their collections and services support these literacies.

## Oral literacy

Within the field of literacy studies, much has been made about the need to take a more global consideration of literacy – to consider, for example, the perception of literacy in those communities where an oral culture dominates. Our survey did not prompt any responses on this subject. However, one of the case study authorities raised the issue of oral literacy, and indicated that they do have a remit to foster and promote it:

> *This estate has been ravaged by the troubles, there is no home environment of books, there is low educational aspiration. There is no bookshop and no book buying tradition. The library works closely with schools in promoting literacy. Here they have access to a free source of information and inspiration. We build on the strong oral tradition that still exists. The children have good listening skills and we connect with these roots by myths, legends and poetry.* (South Eastern Education and Library Board)

This is a matter deserving further consideration, especially in those authorities serving multi-ethnic communities – communities where the oral tradition is endemic.

## Parental involvement and family literacy

Many library authorities emphasized the central importance of facilitating parental involvement in children's reading:

> *Encouraging parents to use the library is vital . . . Parents need to be educated too, about what children read, and how to use the library . . . We can help parents who would be intimidated going into a school to ask what to get for their children.* (Stirling)

One of the major developments within national literacy movements in the past decade has been the emergence of the Family Literacy Initiative run by the Basic Skills Agency and other projects such as the National Literacy Trust's Reading is Fundamental. A number of initiatives run at a local level directly involve the public library service (Taylor, 1999). An important manifestation of this within the public library context has been the Bookstart programmes mentioned earlier (Bray and Ash, 1997; Coleman, 1994). Several library authorities recognized the significance of supporting family literacy, encapsulated in the following extracts:

> *At one level it [family literacy] is about giving children access to a variety of different reading materials, particularly as many children in a city like Birmingham wouldn't have access to those materials through the home environment. They would have access to some via school but in library*

*services we look at education in a slightly different way. In the last few years we have been support-*
*ing the whole family literacy area. One of our strengths in that area, apart from the fact that we work*
*in partnership with others, is that we're providing a context which is not threatening, is non-judg-*
*mental. It is about helping the parents and supporting them no matter how poor their literacy skills*
*are. Making them aware that they do, and can, have a significant impact in developing their children.*
*Most parents with very poor literacy skills want better for their children . . .*

*We are making interventions around family literacy. There is a family literacy strategy which has*
*developed a relationship between libraries and the health authorities. It is difficult to keep promoting*
*literacy when you are looking at poverty and particularly infant mortality, for example. Working*
*more closely with health visitors through the Bookstart project it has become clear that they think lit-*
*eracy is relevant and see it as a crucial part of child development, which they should be involved in.*
(Birmingham)

*We promote adult reading and literature development as a separate entity. But if you say 'Is children's*
*reading related to work in promoting [adult reading skills]?' or rather the other way round 'Do adult*
*reading skills need to be bolstered in supporting children's reading?', there is no doubt. And there are issues*
*around literacy, the issues about confidence. Some parents don't want to read stories to their children*
*because they feel inhibited, but you can encourage parents by working with them and encouraging them to*
*tell stories to their children. The same with adult literacy. Many children that have literacy problems have*
*parents who have literacy problems. You can't separate the two. But we also promote adult reading as a*
*different issue in terms of literature development and as part of that we promote good quality children's*
*literature. That encourages them to read books, but it is not about the reading skill.* (Northamptonshire)

## Support for special needs

Our study was concerned to explore the degree to which children's services offer special support for groups of children with specific reading or learning needs. This is a
field that has received surprisingly scant empirical treatment within the professional
literature in recent years, although the Children's Literature Research Centre at the
Roehampton Institute investigated the reading habits of pupils with special education
needs in their supplementary study set in the school context (British Library Research
and Innovation Centre, 1996).

Figure 2.4 shows a breakdown of provision. The overall figures for support are low,
indicating a need for public libraries to address their responsibilities in this area. The
emphasis is on the blind and partially sighted child, with several libraries indicating
the provision of books for the visually impaired and subscriptions to Clear Vision.

Several libraries stressed the significance of ensuring that children with special needs
were integrated into the main library and benefitted from contact with the broad user
group:

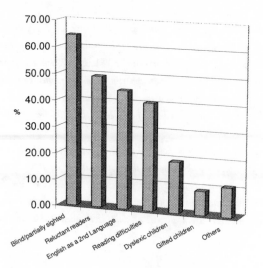

**Fig. 2.4**   *Support for special groups*

*We also work with children with disabilities giving a very strong message that the library has some-thing to offer to all sections of the community. By having a group of able-bodied children in at the same time as a disabled group and having those interactions there is a social message that we give out. Although much of the evidence is anecdotal it does have a benefit to those kids.* (Birmingham)

Two areas of concern are support for dyslexic and gifted children. Recognizing that dyslexia is of particular concern nationally, it is disappointing to note that less than a fifth of respondents appear to make any sort of specific provision. Northamptonshire library service is one of the few surveyed who offer a special collection for dyslexic children. The traditional indifference of public libraries towards acknowledging the needs of the gifted child through targeted collections and services is also reflected in the graph. Birmingham's Centre for the Child was almost alone in mentioning the gifted child:

*There quite rightly is an emphasis at the moment on poor literacy skills and the need to develop skills but we also need to think about the high flyers, how we keep them stimulated.* (Birmingham)

It must be acknowledged, however, that those authorities who do make provision for children with special needs appear deeply committed.

The results pertaining to special needs provision, especially specific learning diffi-culties, may, however, be a reflection of the general ambivalence which public library children's services have towards supporting the formal educational needs of the child.

## Conclusions

Traditionally, the public library has been perceived as a major component in the movement to promote literacy. Within that context, children's libraries have taken as a primary aim the development of reading and the reading habit. However, little was known of their interpretation of literacy. This study offers a much greater delineation of that interpretation, revealing a close concern for instilling a desire and love of reading rather than a formal educational role in inculcating reading skills. Libraries also perceive the importance of reading as contributing to the social and cultural development of the child and seek to facilitate this in different ways.

Literacy is a complex multidimensional concept, and our study demonstrated that children's libraries are becoming alert to their responsibilities to foster the new literacies which embrace traditional non-book materials as well as the new technologies such as the Internet. Whilst commitment to the idea may not yet be matched by actual provision through collections and services, it is gratifying that such vision is spreading. Through this book, we will explore in detail just how children's libraries are fulfilling their responsibility in promoting literacy – of whatever kind – through the development of their collection and programme promotional activities.

On the completion of our study, one county librarian said to me that she was convinced that the time was now ripe for children's libraries to reevaluate their interpretation of literacy and to respond accordingly. This is a worthy sentiment and one that should be pursued with vigour. There are, however, significant educational and training implications inherent in this, which receive further discussion later.

## References

Arjoon, R (1999) Efficient market models: the reality behind economic models in the publishing industry, *Learned Publishing*, **12** (2), 127–33.

Barton, D (1994) *Literacy: an introduction to the ecology of written language*, Blackwell.

Blanshard, C (ed) (1997) *Children and young people: Library Association guidelines for public library services*, 2nd edn, Library Association Publishing.

Bray, C and Ash, J (1997) Bookstart in Wandsworth, *Youth Library Review*, **23** (Spring), 12–14.

British Library Research and Innovation Centre (1996) *Young people's reading at the end of the century*, British Library Research and Innovation Report 14, Children's Literature Research Centre.

Brown, R (1979) Public library aims and objectives: children's services, *Library Association Record*, **81** (8), 382.

Coleman, P (1994) Libraries and literacy: how public libraries should respond. In Barker, K and Lonsdale, R (eds) *Skills for Life?: the meaning and value of literacy: proceedings of the Youth Libraries Group Conference, Mason Hall, University of Birmingham, September 1992*, Taylor-Graham, 75–88.

Denham, D (1997) Children and IT in public libraries: a research project, *Youth Library Review*, **23** (Spring), 20–29.

Elkin, J and Lonsdale, R (1996) *Focus on the child: libraries, literacy and learning*, Library Association Publishing.

Glancy, K (1982) Kids and comics, *Bookmark*, **9**, 11.

Jackson, M (1993) *Literacy*, David Fulton.

Large, J A et al (1994) A comparison of information retrieval from print and CD-ROM versions of an encyclopedia by elementray school students, *Information Processing and Management*, **30** (4), 499–513.

Library and Information Services Council (England) Working Party on Library Services to Children and Young People (1995) *Investing in children: the future of library services for children and young people*, HMSO.

Library Association (1991) *Children and young people: Library Association guidelines for public library services*, Library Association Publishing.

Lonsdale, R and Wheatley, A (1990) *Provision of audiovisual and computer materials to young people by British public libraries*, BNB Research Fund 49,The British Library.

McGarry, K J (1994) Definitions and meanings of literacy. In Barker, K and Lonsdale, R (eds) *Skills for Life?: the meaning and value of literacy: proceedings of the Youth Libraries Group Conference, Mason Hall, University of Birmingham, September 1992*, Taylor Graham, 3–17.

Meek, M (1991) *On being literate*, The Bodley Head.

Meyer, N J (1994) Hypertext and its role in reading, *Journal of Youth Services in Libraries*, **7** (2), (Winter), 133–9.

Moon, C (1977) Comic comments: constructive uses of comic techniques, *Junior Education*, **1** (May), 27.

Nielsen, J (1997) How users read on the web, *Alertbox*, (October) (available at **http://www.useit.com/alertbox/9710a.html**).

Taylor, C (1999) Read on – write away!: developing community literacy projects in libraries, *Youth Library Review*, **26**, (Spring), 12–13.

Willinsky, J (1990) *The new literacy: redefining reading and writing in schools*, Routledge.

Wray, D et al (1989) *Literacy in action*, The Falmer Press.

# CHAPTER 3

# The clients and partners

Debbie Denham

> Every child has a right to quality public services, whatever their educational talent, whatever the richness of the family background. Everybody needs libraries. (Head of library service)

## Introduction

The previous chapters looked at the context within which library services for children are currently operating and the role of children's libraries in supporting literacy. This chapter moves on to discuss the nature and range of children's library service clients. These include the individual child as well as parents, teachers, carers and other adults concerned with children's reading.

The nationwide survey undertaken for A Place for Children asked library authorities to identify the ages and categories of children as well as adults whom they saw as their key clients and how they identified their role in children's reading. A distinction was made between children as individuals and children in groups, to discover whether there was a significant difference in library service provision. This was supplemented with evidence gathered in the case studies. Respondents were asked to identify the age groups and categories of children on which reading promotional activities were focused and the perceived benefits of the library to children. They provided evidence which demonstrated the role of the library in promoting children's reading to different client groups.

## The individual child

In *Focus on the child*, Elkin and Lonsdale attempted to define the nature and characteristics of the child in the UK at the end of the 20th century. They asked the question:

Is he or she:

- a child of the city; a child of the country?
- wealthy; poverty stricken?
- living within a warm family environment, perhaps with a large extended family and lots of siblings; a child with a single parent, step parents, grandparents, adoptive parents, a gay couple?
- a secure, loved child; an insecure abused child?
- able-bodied; singly or multiply-handicapped; a child with sensory impairment; a child in hospital?
- a young person who is homeless, a child of a homeless family?
- a child who appears to have suffered or is likely to suffer significant harm; whose emotional development has been impaired?
- a child in care?
- a child of a travelling family? (Elkin and Lonsdale, 1996, 1–2)

They provided a picture of children showing considerable diversity and complexity:

The child may be any of the above and in addition:

- live in very varied geographical areas, rural or urban, flat or mountainous, in England, Ireland, Scotland or Wales, with very different local or national traditions, cultures and languages;
- be part of the 'North–South' divide, which separates the more privileged south from the traditionally less privileged rest of the UK.

A further dimension is added by the broadening nature of the UK population, with immigration over recent decades from every part of the world, but particularly from the English-speaking Commonwealth countries. Thus the UK child:

- may originate from cultures very different from traditional UK cultures, from Africa, the Caribbean, the Indian sub-continent, the Middle East, the Far East;
- may belong to any of a variety of religions, eg Anglican, Buddhist, Catholic, Hindu, Jewish, Muslim, Sikh;
- may speak languages other than English as his or her mother tongue or community language, particularly Urdu, Punjabi, Bengali, Vietnamese, Mandarin, or European languages, eg French, Spanish, Greek, Italian. (Elkin and Lonsdale, 1996, 1–2)

As is suggested above, public library services and resources must be tailored to meet the individual as well as the collective needs of the child. *Investing in children* also recognized the diversity and individuality of children:

Needs for, and expectations of, a library service are conditioned by age, developmental stage, ability, the special needs of disadvantaged or minority groups, and by conditioning factors such as home circumstances or distance from a library. It is important that the public library in particular which caters for all age groups, should be able to recognise the different needs arising at different ages and stages of development and should strive to satisfy these in appropriate ways . . . recognition of these needs should inform and determine the aims and objectives of all libraries that serve this client group . . . We believe that the needs of the individuals within this group [children 0–16] for books, for libraries and for encouragement of reading and the use of information, should be the starting point for any consideration of library services delivered to them. (LISC(E), 1995, 5)

## Key clients

Our study asked heads of children's library services to define their key clients in relation to the development of reading. Questions elicited information on categories of children and concerned adults whom they perceived as their key clients. These were split into specific groups, by age and role:

- Pre-school
- 5–9, 10–11, 12–14, 15–16
- children not in school
- parents
- pre-school carers
- primary teachers
- secondary teachers
- other professionals.

Respondents were asked to identify how significant specific client groups were in terms of children's reading and to identify whether the perception of service to these clients was focused on individuals or collectively as part of a specific group.

## Children

The majority of authorities considered that individual children in all age categories between pre-school and 16 were key clients, with a slight reduction at the age of 15 in Northern Ireland and Wales. Secondary-aged school children as individuals rather than as groups were more likely to be considered as important clients. This reflected the tendency of the library service to attempt to disassociate itself from schools when dealing with teenagers, in the belief that teenagers will be less receptive if the library service is too closely linked to the school environment, but the concentration appears to be on younger (11–14) rather than older (15+) teenagers.

Children (0–11years) in groups were also seen as a significant element of children's library service. This was reduced when secondary-aged school children (12–16) were considered as a group. Very few authorities saw groups of over-fives as key clients outside the school environment, the priority clearly being seen to serve children in groups through their schools. This suggested that travelling children and home-educated children were not reached as effectively as children in school. This may be accounted for by the difficulty of accessing such children; there is a relatively 'captive audience' for libraries of all children aged 5–16 if sufficiently good links are developed with local schools. This is far harder to achieve with children who are not schooled within mainstream education.

Respondents were asked to highlight the most significant categories of clients in terms of children's reading. Again children were considered as individuals and in groups. Under-fives were acknowledged as being the most important. This supports the considerable energy and endeavour currently being used in reaching children at this early age. Responses suggested that recent initiatives such as Bookstart were a priority for developing services. Secondary-aged school children (12–16) as a group were not identified by respondents as important in terms of reading in comparison to other age groups and to 12–16-year-olds as individuals.

## Pre-school

In the research undertaken during the case studies, interviewees were also asked to identify key clients in relation to children's reading. A similar pattern emerged with *all* children identified as key clients by librarians:

> We serve all ages, 0–14, promoting awareness of books, developing literacy and language skills, and encouraging independent study. (Hampshire)

Many library authorities recognized that, although all children were clients, for a variety of pragmatic and ethical reasons it was necessary to focus energies into serving children in particular age groups:

> Philosophically we serve all. Practically it is easier to get to the under fives. It is always difficult to find books appealing to boys of 11+. In a way the publishing field influences our priorities. (Southampton)

> I think it must be early years, mustn't it? That is always, always, always the key emphasis . . . But at the same time we are trying to move onwards to the older child, or indeed the young person and that is why we appointed a youth librarian before we had a youth library, working with young people aged between 13 and 18 largely. It seems to me we cannot afford to let them down at a time when they are the most intensive users of libraries. We do not see 16 and 17 year olds, they are quite

*invisible in their use, but they are still there. I think in this we had to start somewhere, so we said we will focus on these younger children, but as they grow up you have got to provide services for teenagers. But if I could only serve one client group, there is absolutely no doubt in my mind it would be the under sevens actually, because in learning to read they are assimilating everything they need for life and it will make a difference.* (Leeds)

*We aim to serve all children, but see that the public library is unique where pre-school children are concerned: it can be the most significant stimulus to reading these children have.* (Croydon)

**One head of library services emphasized:**

*The early literacy, pre-reading skills I see as absolutely crucial. We have always given them a lot of priority in the allocation of resources and energy.*

*Pre-school is very important. If we can get them at that level hopefully we will stay with them. It's a bit more difficult because you have to capture the parents. The children love books automatically so you have no problems capturing them and their attention but obviously you need parents to bring them in.* (Birmingham)

Under-fives were also recognized as important in a group situation. Much of the outreach work which takes place from children's libraries is focused on the under-fives:

*We encourage playgroups to come to the library, and we visit playgroups in turn.* (Northamptonshire)

## Early school years

Children during their first years at school were also viewed as key clients. Children learning to read need the support which can be provided by the library service to supplement and improve emerging reading skills, and a number of heads of library services recognized this, whilst trying to keep a balance in library provision:

*There is a primary age (or even younger) bias in the service, which is instinctive (rather than accidental); it corresponds with the missionary aim to get them hooked while they're young. There are no other groups specially targeted, and there is no staff expertise which might predispose a targeted service for one particular group.*

*There is a primary age bias in the services but no groups are excluded from it. An attempt to make the most effective use of limited resources in attracting younger children and making life-long users out of them.* (Neath Port Talbot)

Some authorities had taken the challenge of meeting the needs of this client group further, with one authority creating a half-time post specifically for early-years work. Clear, rationalized views were expressed on the need to focus services on particular age groups and on the reasons why the younger age group was the most vital in terms of service provision:

> *At the moment we limit our class visits to infants and Year 3 on the grounds that we need to encourage that familiarity with libraries, familiarity with reading books for fun at a young age. That is also the reason we have under fives sessions. In the slightly older age range we also have a bit of a drive on teenagers.* (Southwark)

> *Class visits are made by primary schools, but rarely secondary schools. Although our aim is to work with schools throughout the borough, there is a temptation to work with the keen ones. We see class visits as a powerful tool for us. We have a specific policy about informing schools of public library opportunities.* (Croydon)

## Groups

> *We play quite a pro-active role. We have identified specific areas to work at to make contact with pre-school children, mothers and toddlers, playgroups, brownies, infant schools and so on. We encourage schools to come and visit the library, although success often depends on the attitude of the school's head. We tend to target a particular area and work on that. Quite often this will be schools within walking distance.* (Northamptonshire)

Occasionally someone queried whether libraries are actually providing what children want, suggesting that there are some children whom the library will inevitably never reach:

> *Many initiatives by children's librarians during the 1990s have talked directly to the library client, but 'real' kids do not necessarily want to read for their leisure and so they do not come to the library.*

## Special needs

A number of library authorities made provision for children with special needs. The questionnaire asked respondents to identify specific support offered for special reading needs through the provision of targeted collections or services. Support for children who were blind or partially sighted was provided by a majority of the authorities as indicated in Table 3.1.

**Table 3.1**  *Percentage of respondents with targeted services/collections*

| | Reading difficulties | English as second language | Reluctant readers | Gifted children | Dyslexia | Blind/ partial sight | Other | Number of respondents |
|---|---|---|---|---|---|---|---|---|
| Counties | 39 | 61 | 48 | 13 | 30 | 83 | 4 | 23 |
| Metropolitan districts | 52 | 44 | 48 | 4 | 12 | 68 | 16 | 25 |
| London | 39 | 69 | 58 | 15 | 23 | 50 | 19 | 26 |
| Unitary authorities | 37 | 47 | 42 | 0 | 11 | 74 | 5 | 19 |
| Wales | 25 | 20 | 45 | 5 | 10 | 60 | 10 | 20 |
| Scotland | 46 | 35 | 54 | 15 | 27 | 62 | 12 | 26 |
| NI | 75 | 0 | 75 | 0 | 25 | 75 | 0 | 4 |
| UK | 41 | 46 | 50 | 9 | 20 | 66 | 11 | 143 |

Specific support for dyslexic children was offered only by a relatively small percentage of authorities (20%). Gifted children were particularly poorly served by library authorities, with only 9% offering specific support. Was this the result of a lack of understanding of the nature of support needed by the children or is it based on the assumption that they will already receive adequate support elsewhere, in the home and school environment?

As a number of librarians said:

*We always give a lot of priority to children with special needs or children in need. That takes a variety of forms but specifically children with learning difficulties.* (Birmingham)

*There was a period of outreach activities at a school for severely learning-handicapped children, but it was less successful than it could have been because the library staff members were untrained in how to work with these children.*

Support for special services and meeting the needs of particular clients can be improved by the provision of staff with specific skills:

*We have staff with specialist skills, eg a member of staff who is deaf tells stories at a local school for deaf children.*

Teachers also recognized early support to children with special needs as important in the social context:

*Libraries are a facility where mainstream children go and so special needs children can mix with other children there and learn about how to behave in the library environment. It also introduces special needs children to an important community facility.* (Birmingham)

## Reluctant readers

Boys who were reluctant readers, often during their teenage years, were identified as a group where special provision needed to be made, although little appeared to have been done in the area:

*We have often done things around teenagers but perhaps we need to be more focused, eg boys where there is reading failure. I can see where that tips over into the Adult Education Service, when young men are presenting themselves for basic skills sessions, or not, as the case may be.*

*Children who can read but don't particularly want to, especially boys . . . We need to do more although we are beginning to do it now working with the play and youth service.*

## Home-educated children

One authority was particularly concerned to try to meet the needs of children who were being educated at home, through providing access to a range of resources to support their learning:

*One of the areas where we have been making a significant impact is the whole area of home education. For many families and kids the mainstream education system does not work for them or is not what they are looking for. The library service can have a direct benefit because we can provide material, resources, facilities, activities and services specifically targeting home education.* (Birmingham)

## Ethnic minority groups

There was some limited targeting of specific services to meet the needs of a range of ethnic groups within the local community. A number of authorities identified the benefits of doing so:

*A community resource for children. The Bangladeshi community doesn't use the library much, but their children are using it now. It provides an important route to language integration/social integration for ethnic minorities in particular.*

*Those children in the black community who are failing I would like to see as a priority but not because they are black but because like other white children the education system is failing them. A lot of par-*

*ents are desperate to make sure their children do not fail and I am sure we have a role to play there, particularly around reading.*

## Gifted children

As well as children who need support for poor reading skills and low levels of literacy, one librarian identified the need to provide support for children who are high achievers:

> *There quite rightly is an emphasis at the moment on poor literacy skills and the need to develop skills but we also need to think about the high flyers, how we keep them stimulated.* (Birmingham)

There was a general recognition of the need to target services, as a proactive method of delivering high-quality services to clearly identified groups or areas of users. It was seen as both providing a focus and allowing resources to be concentrated on areas where the greatest need had been identified:

> *There is a big divide between areas of the city in what is needed and how children and parents behave. Targeting is therefore essential.* (Edinburgh)

## Adults

All types of library authorities considered that adults as well as children were their clients although authorities varied as to the importance they accorded adults. Parents as individuals were recognized by over 95% of authorities as key clients. This pattern was reinforced when libraries identified the significance of parents' contribution to children's reading. Parents as individuals were seen as very important in terms of children's reading but much less important in groups. This may again be a question of access; it is difficult to access parents in groups. Despite a number of library authorities offering family reading sessions and outreach visits to under-fives playgroups, the majority of parents visit the library on an individual basis.

Other adults identified as key clients included teachers and other professionals. Preschool carers were seen as particularly significant in all types of authority, reflected in the considerable work carried out by library authorities with under-fives groups. In Northern Ireland primary school teachers were highlighted as being significantly more important than secondary school teachers; this may reflect the different structure of library services in Northern Ireland, where libraries are integrated with education in education and library boards. When these adults were considered in relation to their significance in terms of reading, a similar pattern was repeated, with pre-school and primary school teachers being considered as most important, after parents, while secondary school teachers and other professionals were seen as having less significance.

These findings suggest that, although children are the libraries' key clients, it is often necessary to access them through an adult, and that working with a wide range of adults and professional carers will enhance the quality of the service available to the individual child.

It was also perceived as vital for parents to be educated in the range of books available and how to use them with their children:

*We have to educate the parents too, about the importance of the library.*

At the same time they also acknowledged the need to encourage children and parents who are *not* currently library users:

*The people who do not join the library in this area are the ones who are scared of libraries and you really need to promote libraries to the parents there.*

*More non book-oriented parents need to be encouraged, but that creates problems.*

*One of our aims is to ensure as many children as possible use the library and as many children as possible join the library. We know that many children use us but don't actually take books out although they use us for all sorts of other purposes.*

## Customer focus

There was an increasing focus on customers and determining their service needs:

*It's a very child oriented service. There is a commitment to children in our policy document and that's followed through in stock selection and in-service training. We give a high priority to ensuring a positive attitude to children, and to providing them with appropriate materials.* (South Eastern Education and Library Board)

The importance of children and teenagers experiencing a sense of ownership of the library was also reinforced:

*It is very important that children feel valued and they won't if you give them old bookstock and just assume you know what is best. A branch library was refurbished with input from children and that really helps them see that the library is their library.* (Southwark)

*The teenage reading group is their session, their choice, so they get a say in which magazines we get, what snacks we buy. With the teenage reading group also we have promoted a strong group identity.* (Southwark)

## Customer surveys

The need for customer surveys was clearly articulated:

*We can benefit children by asking them what they want from libraries. We want to talk to as many as we can and with the youngest children informal conversations with the parents and carers of the under fives are very important.*

*People use libraries for an awful lot of reasons. There was a library service in the North West who three years ago surveyed their readers and found that over half their readers who came into libraries didn't borrow a book.*

Although surveys of customers are becoming more common, it is evident that there is still a need to undertake such surveys in a systematic and logical way to allow for optimum benefits. As one parent pointed out:

*. . . a library survey . . . was conducted a while back when [a local library] was under threat of closure. It was useless because it was only done in the library, where many people who would like to use it do not go for a variety of reasons. The questionnaire should have been put through everybody's door to get an idea of what all the local residents think.*

Statistics gained from such a survey could provide a distorted view and if used to determine changes in service provision could lead to a service which is not responsive to the needs of users and prospective users. The development of the CIPFA Children's PLUS survey (CIPFA, 1998) will provide opportunities for libraries to take a more systematic view of children's opinions and requirements. Children's PLUS has produced a standard survey methodology which all library authorities can use to identify customer needs as perceived by the children themselves:

*We will start using Children's PLUS next year as soon as it is out. That does go beyond outputs, we are going to get into consumers' opinions of us and that in itself will give us a measure of impact. The kids themselves will be telling us what they like, don't like and what they are getting out of the library service. Children rarely get a voice of that kind.*

## Added value

A range of intangible social benefits were associated with library service provision, particularly the fact that the public library service is free and available to all:

*. . . the library is open to everybody although I think we still don't reach some of the children we want to reach as much as we would like.*

One parent emphasized the freedom this brought:

> *I find that free access to large numbers of books extends my choice, and it doesn't matter so much if we choose a book and don't like it. I value libraries for the scope to make mistakes and different choices.*

The provision of a welcoming and non-threatening environment was also seen as a prime value of the library to its users:

> *This is a warm safe place where children learn a sense of ownership.*

> *We try to make it a comfortable place for them, away from restrictions like 'don't touch, don't speak'.*

> *We're providing a context which is not threatening, non-judgmental. It is about helping the parents and supporting them no matter how poor their literacy skills are. Making them aware that they do, and can, have a significant impact in developing their children.*

The library can be seen to have a role as an agent to counteract social exclusion. Specific benefits for children were identified as:

> *Reading develops social awareness and the library provides children with a rare opportunity to choose for themselves and opportunity for self-expression and discrimination. They have a unique freedom to do what they want.* (Southampton)

> *We offer children a first right of citizenship. We are the first statutory service that the kids get and we offer them the library membership card which belongs to them, the first thing they own for themselves.* (Birmingham)

## Marketing

There has been some resistance within library services to take on board the full implications of developing marketing and business strategies. This reluctance has often stemmed from the concept of libraries as a service industry and therefore not in the business of 'selling a product'. In fact libraries have always 'sold' services and the benefits of those services to their users (Kinnell and MacDougall, 1994). Once there is acceptance of the need to market services it is imperative that librarians develop strategies to inform and direct their energies in understanding and meeting client needs. Over the last ten to fifteen years there has been an increasing emphasis on the customer and the identification of the customer's needs. In libraries this has led to a shift in emphasis away from stock to focusing on the users themselves and the demands they will place on the stock. There has also been a changing terminology which encourages librarians to look at 'users' rather than 'borrowers'. As the range of provision made by libraries continues to diversify, particularly in the field of information and communications technology (ICT), increasingly library users may not be traditional borrowers.

Another marketing concept which is being embraced by public libraries is that of customer responsiveness. In relation to children, this has resulted in the production of CIPFA's Children's PLUS survey (CIPFA, 1998) mentioned above. The move towards a more client-focused approach to the delivery of library services is fraught with problems in relation to children's services – eg obtaining permission from parents to interview children – but well worth the effort involved.

## Targeting

Although there is general acceptance that all children are the clients, it is evident that services are increasingly being targeted to meet the needs of particular client groups at any one time. There is an emphasis on targeting of provision rather than blanket provision to all. A realistic way of managing decreasing budgets, and increasing pressures on services and staff, is to provide a focus for expenditure, probably on the basis of a rolling programme. The literature provides support for the concept of focusing on particular groups of users, identifying their needs and marketing services to meet these needs specifically. Catherine Blanshard offers an example of how local authority swimming pools have addressed this:

> To begin with it was invariably marketed as a swimming pool for all. When local authorities began to identify features which would benefit specific areas of the community, such as ladies' nights, toddlers' sessions and family swimming, they began to target or segment users. The organizers then went on to identify the benefits of using the pool in this way. Ladies' nights were marketed as a time to swim safely and in peace. The up-turn in use as a result of splitting users into groups and aiming marketing specifically at each group is now legend. (Blanshard, 1998, 47)

Another reason for targeting services is pragmatic:

> It can be argued that it is especially necessary in the area of leisure and library services to adopt an approach of target group definition. These services have a broad-based product and therefore a very wide potential market. It is impossible, both economically and practically, to provide a comprehensive service to the entire community. Limited resources imply the need to offer particular value-added services to a set of clearly defined target groups (for example, the disabled, local businesses, and ethnic minority groups), while a wide-ranging basic service is offered to the community as a whole. (Kinnell and MacDougall, 1994, 96)

This would allow for the general provision of books and other resources for loan and reference within the library, but for outreach services, special reading groups and in-library events to be targeted to specific priority groups. It is evident that libraries are doing this but they have not yet all taken the step of effectively marketing the benefits of service initiatives to their target audiences.

## Staff training and attitudes

When attempting to develop and operate a customer-focused environment for service delivery, it is vital for staff to be adequately and effectively trained. They particularly need customer-care training and an understanding of child development. The continued need for training in these areas was identified in the questionnaire and case study surveys. Although customer-care training is offered in the majority of authorities (see Figure 3.1), child-development training is much less likely to be offered, even though a considerable number of authorities identify it as being beneficial (see Figure 3.2).

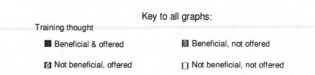

Key to all graphs:

Training thought
■ Beneficial & offered                ▨ Beneficial, not offered
▨ Not beneficial, offered          □ Not beneficial, not offered

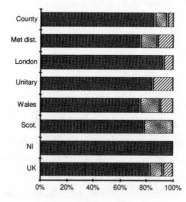

**Fig. 3.1** *Importance ratings for, and number of authorities who offer, customer-care training*

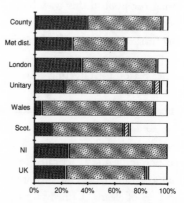

**Fig. 3.2** *Importance ratings for, and number of authorities who offer, child-development training*

## Partnerships

In delivering services to a range of clients, it is increasingly important for libraries to be aware of the range of potential partners coupled with a need to access funding opportunities to support service development. Some key partners are discussed in Chapter 5.

## Local authority partners

Librarians saw the lack of, or poor nature of, internal local government links and cooperation as a factor which had changed little over recent years. Some authorities have obviously made headway, the links between Birmingham's Director of Libraries and Adult Education and its Director of Education being exemplary. This kind of partnership has not been achieved, however, without considerable input on the part of the people involved, and it has to be recognized that this is usually initiated by the library personnel rather than coming from other agencies, as one authority suggested:

> *I do not think there is anybody we do not co-operate with.*

Once these relationships have been developed, the library service often becomes a key partner or leader in strategy and policy development, but some authorities still found it hard to make links with key local authority departments concerned with children and their welfare. Libraries, although they see themselves as obvious players, are too often left out of appropriate teams, and are not being proposed as partners when new initiatives are proposed in the local arena. Many library authorities are not included in any literacy development work:

> *The Education Department is working on promoting reading and information skills and we would love to be in on the planning, but it hasn't happened, yet all we do for children is linked with that. Things are changing slowly. The Chief Executive is interested in our work. Our opinion is now being asked.*

> *The link between libraries and literacy hasn't been made.*

Libraries need to establish their credibility and often have to fight extremely hard to achieve this. In a number of authorities it was acknowledged that the relationship between the education department and the library service was rather fragile, fraught with tensions. Often the library service was the key instigator of contact but was rebuffed by the education department and its interest was not reciprocated. In some authorities the problem had been recognized at corporate level and considerable effort had been applied to improving internal links across the council:

*Our new Chief Executive seems to realise the importance of the public library's role, especially its critical input for pre-school children.*

*It would be quite difficult now to set up a family literacy initiative with one of those partners [libraries, education and adult education] missing even though their roles are very different.*

In Leeds an innovative scheme exists where monies saved from direct-debit council tax payments were targeted for literacy development work. Despite such innovation there is still the plea:

*There are people we would like to get more noticed by as a key deliverer of literacy and children's reading.*

Using local community volunteers to support reading, largely through schools, has become more widespread. Leeds has a 'Help a child to read' project and Birmingham also has a reading volunteers scheme where volunteers work in schools but are trained by library staff.

The youth service may appear to be a key local authority partner as it too provides an informal environment for young people. However, it is often difficult to develop relationships:

*We find the youth service a bit impenetrable because by their nature they try to look detached from the local authority, they have to maintain their street cred.*

Many library services still work closely with the schools library service, but changes in funding and structure of schools library services has caused the relationship with these traditional partners to become increasingly tense and difficult to manage. This is a distressing result of changes in educational policy, where natural partners in the promotion of reading may have become protectively territorial in order to survive.

## Schools

There was a strong feeling that schools are and need to be key partners because of the ease and benefit of accessing the majority of children via schools:

*You can't work without the education sector.*

*We haven't an institutional raft for adults of the kind school visits provide.*

There is a clear dichotomy in the relationship with schools which has been reflected in public libraries for many years now. There is an issue as to whether to focus on class visits to the library, offering information skills, book talks and book changing sessions within the library environment, or to reach a wider number of schools and take on a more promotional role, talking about books, encouraging reading, storytelling, in the school environment. The library service still needs to realize fully the potential for reaching children through schools. There are formal links in terms of class visits and booktalks, but there is also the possibility of a less formal relationship, where schools might operate as a promotional outlet for the library service.

It is clear that many teachers do recognize the important role the library has in the reading life of the child. The greater awareness of the valuable support libraries provide for reading and literacy was demonstrated in one authority by one primary school paying for three hours of library staff time to cover more visits – this in an authority where there is no bookshop and no book-buying tradition. Adding credence to the avowal that the library is a social force of importance.

It is of considerable concern, however, to encounter teachers who still feel that:

*We don't hear about [library] activities.*

*. . . the library doesn't inform us about events.*

Many authorities identified their strategy as one of working either directly with schools or through the aegis of the schools library service, rather than directly approaching the education department and convincing staff there of the worth of libraries. Cooperation tended to be at grass roots level rather than strategic. Many teachers interviewed recognized the role of the library in children's reading development and stressed the complementary role of education and libraries. Not all saw this picture, however, and there are still primary school teachers who believe that:

*The school plants the seed of reading.*

This demonstrates a lack of understanding of the work which librarians (and parents) do to introduce children to books and reading. The seeds of reading are hopefully sown long before children reach school:

*It has been proven beyond doubt that children who are encouraged to read in their pre-school years and early school years, by parents and carers in the home, by teachers, and by librarians in the school and the public library, have a considerable advantage in terms of educational performance and later achievement over those who have not been provided with these opportunities.* (Aslib, 1995, 11)

Cooperative ventures arise between schools and the library. This is one aspect of the service severely affected by cutbacks, with branches no longer able to spare staff to visit local schools.

## Conclusions

Surveys carried out for A Place for Children identified how library services are targeting their services to meet the needs of specific client groups. Libraries are also utilizing key marketing concepts to determine the direction of service development. Key clients in terms of reading development are identified as the under-fives and emergent readers in schools. This raises concern as to whether libraries are underselling older children. Although there is no question of the importance of supporting and nurturing pre-reading and emergent reading skills, there is a need to reinforce and build on these skills throughout the life of the child. This research also demonstrated an awareness on the part of librarians of the vital role which contact with parents and teachers plays in accessing children, particularly at the younger end of the age range, as well as the parents' awareness of the library as a safe and empowering place. There is still considerable scope for libraries to provide more targeted support for a variety of children's reading needs. This could perhaps be improved by raising awareness through staff training and the identification and purchase of suitable resources. (Chapter 4 assesses collection development.)

## References

Aslib (1995) *Review of public library services in England and Wales for the Department of National Heritage*, Aslib.

Blanshard, C (1998) *Managing library services for children and young people: a practical handbook*, Library Association Publishing.

CIPFA (1998) *Children's PLUS: a national standard for surveying children and young people in public libraries and the community*, British Library Research and Innovation Centre Institute of Public Finance.

Elkin, J and Lonsdale, R (1996) *Focus on the child: libraries, literacy and learning*, Library Association Publishing.

Kinnell, M and MacDougall, J (1994) *Meeting the marketing challenge: strategies for public libraries and leisure services*, Taylor Graham.

Library and Information Services Council (England) Working Party on Library Services for Children and Young People (1995) *Investing in children: the future of library services for children and young people*, Library Information Series 22, HMSO.

CHAPTER 4

# Collection development and reading

## Ray Lonsdale

> Arguably one of the most important responsibilities of the librarian (indeed, among the greatest arts that librarians possess) is that of planning, building, maintaining and promoting a dynamic and pertinent collection. (Elkin and Lonsdale, 1996)

## Introduction

Collection development is the generic term commonly used to denote those responsibilities set out in the quotation above, and it embraces an array of complex activities and procedures. It is perhaps worth rehearsing what these procedures comprise, since a myth abounds in the profession that collection development is simply synonymous with the selection and acquisition of new stock. This is not the case. Collection development involves a number of other elements:

- the evaluation and acquisition of donations and gifts
- the creation of in-house material designed to serve the specific needs of a particular library or user group (particularly relevant in school libraries and some school library services)
- collection evaluation and collection review (weeding, the replacement of stock, relegation of materials)
- preservation and conservation, and the various means of promoting the collection.

During the past decade there has been a recognition that these procedures are as apposite for the virtual collection as for the resources physically held within a specific library. Increasingly, the wealth of materials accessed via the Internet or held within other libraries is being made available to young people, their parents and carers, and thus the activities of collection management must embrace these resources too.

Although this is a new manifestation of collection development, academic libraries in North America have already created taxonomies of Internet resources that define the range of virtual materials which the library wishes to make available to users and the degree to which this material is networked within the library system. There is as yet little evidence of such taxonomies within the children's library field but such developments are inevitable.

For the various activities of collection development to be undertaken in a coordinated and consistent manner, a systematic programme needs to be established based upon an agreed, pragmatic and ideally written policy statement – a sentiment which is reflected in the Library Association guidelines (Library Association, 1991; Blanshard, 1997).

Our study set out to explore the role of collection management in supporting the reading needs of the child; something which, to our knowledge, had not before been investigated empirically. We began by considering the synergy which exists between on the one hand the philosophies held by libraries on reading and literacy and on the other hand the aims and objectives of their collection policy statements.

## Collection development policies and reading

Contrary to the beliefs held within the professional literature that a written policy statement is critical for the successful development of a collection, earlier studies of public library services to children and young people in the UK revealed that comparatively few British children's libraries had produced a formal written policy (Lonsdale and Wheatley, 1990; Lonsdale and Everitt, 1996). Whilst authorities did sometimes produce informal policies, the literature suggested that many did not acknowledge the existence of non-book materials, in particular electronic materials, within the collection, or the issue of the virtual library (Lonsdale and Wheatley, 1990) – an issue which has relevance for the new literacies.

Almost half of the respondents in our study indicated that they possessed a written collection policy, signifying an increase since the earlier studies mentioned above. However, when we explored whether library authorities had established a specific collection policy statement that addressed children's reading, a mere 8% of respondents indicated that they possessed such a policy. Whilst it may be argued that consideration of children's reading might be accommodated within a general written policy document for collection management, that less than half of the respondents possess such a document reveals the lack of formal consideration being given to this issue.

## Collection policy statements

Many of the policy documents that we analysed did not conform to the traditional models, and appeared to centre solely on the selection and acquisition of new materials. A major component was a detailed statement of the range of selection criteria. Those few that did set out their objectives revealed a strong sense that the authority was seeking to link the stated philosophy on reading and literacy with the collection development process. Frequently, these statements reflected the prevalent view on reading discussed in Chapter 2, which emphasized the library's role in inculcating a belief in the value of reading, the pleasures of reading or the relevance of reading to the social and cultural and emotional development of the child. One such example is taken from Essex:

*Public Library Stock Selection Policy*

*The Aims and Objectives of the Children's Service are described in full in Policy Statement D1 but are introduced here in order to demonstrate their relevance to resource provision.*

- *To provide a comprehensive and efficient library service, delivered at a professional standard by all staff to children, their parents and carers.*
- *To ensure that facilities are available for the borrowing of or reference to books and other materials sufficient in number, range and quality to meet the general requirements and any special requirements of children.*
- *To encourage all children and their parents and carers to use libraries and to provide advice as to their use and any other information required.*
- *To ensure that all the available resources are used in the most effective way.*
- *To encourage a belief in the value and enjoyment of reading among children and the adults who care for, and work with them.*

*The stock selected must support these objectives by actively encouraging all children to enjoy books and reading. It is also important for the service to recognise that every child has a relatively unknown potential for personal development. It is therefore our particular responsibility to ensure that all children have the opportunity to find their own level and to explore and choose from collections representing the whole range of children's literature.*

Those authorities who identified the inculcation of reading skills as a specific objective usually did not elaborate how they would facilitate this, either in terms of the range of stock which was made available to children, or in the activities that would be undertaken. One wonders whether such statements simply constituted platitudes, albeit sincere ones.

There were occasional examples of decisions being taken which reflected the linking of stock to reading methods. For example, Bedford's policy statement states that:

*Stock promotion will revolve around activities that stimulate children's language development, interest in books, reading . . .*

Later in the policy document, there is a delineation of types of stock, and under the section 'Beginning to read' a statement is included to the effect that:

> . . . *paired reading books enabling parent and child to share the reading experience should also feature.*

The extensive lists of selection criteria contained within most policy documents suggest that children's librarians are addressing a comprehensive and penetrating set of issues during the selection process. There is comprehensive coverage of traditional issues relating to the intellectual and physical make-up of fiction and non-fiction books. Political correctness and intellectual freedom are regularly included, and a number of statements set out separate lists of criteria for certain user groups, most particularly the younger child (Bury, Bournemouth and Lambeth) and teenagers (Bury, Redcar and Cleveland).

The most striking omission throughout the policy statements that we scrutinized concerns specific selection criteria for non-book materials and electronic resources in particular – a significant finding in earlier research (Lonsdale and Wheatley, 1990). Almost eight years on, there is little evidence that the issue is being addressed, although there have been significant developments in the provision of electronic materials and we are on the threshold of the instigation of the People's Network. Anecdotal evidence suggests that there is an ignorance about evaluating and selecting material such as CD-ROMs and resources on the Internet – something which the Youth Libraries Group of The Library Association is addressing with its projected publications programme. One of its new series of practical guides will be about the evaluation and quality control of websites and others will follow on related ICT themes.

## The composition of the collection
### Reading-scheme materials

An analysis of the attitudes of librarians towards the provision of materials to support children's reading, and of actual provision, suggested that several striking conclusions may be drawn. Public libraries do not believe that they have a responsibility to offer reading-scheme materials, and neither do they make this literature available to any significant degree (only 20% of respondents make this material available). The low status accorded to reading-scheme materials is reflected in the provision of National Curriculum materials in general, with only 42% of children's library services currently including them in their collections. As regards the availability of this material across authorities, our study suggests that provision in the London boroughs was above average.

Few libraries offered a rationale for this, although one authority proffered the following insight, which is in sympathy with the views postulated in the literature about school and societal literacy (Barton, 1994):

> *There is a whole agenda around literacy in education, which is too narrowly defined. Competence is only one criterion. Reading is about more than just reading schemes. We have a role in broadening perceptions of what reading and imagination is about. I think we have a campaigning role.*
> (Northamptonshire)

## Non-book materials

Despite the emphasis on supporting visual literacy, and the professional literature which indicates the significant contribution which comics can make to supporting children's reading (Glancy, 1982; Moon, 1977), this particular form of material is also largely under-represented in respondents' collections (36%). Magazines (71%) and newspapers (77%), two of the traditional formats, are represented in most responding authorities, while the enthusiasm and concern for graphic novels is now manifest in their extensive inclusion within children's and teenagers' collections (82%).

The evidence from previous studies into the provision of audiovisual and electronic materials suggests that a high degree of importance is accorded to the role of talking books in supporting children's reading (Lonsdale and Wheatley, 1991; Denham, 1997). The findings of our study corroborate these earlier conclusions, and the very high incidence of provision of talking books (97%) confirms that they remain a significant element of children's collections. Whilst an equally high value is placed on special-needs talking books by librarians who responded to our questionnaire, only 65% of respondents make provision in this area. There is anecdotal evidence to suggest that talking books not only play an important role in encouraging the reading habit of all children, but that they have a specific contribution to make for those children who have specific learning difficulties and for whom print-based material can be seen as something of an anathema. We also perceive an ambivalence towards the value of language-teaching tapes. Sixty per cent of respondents accorded it a low to medium value, yet this is not borne out in the collection statistics, with 82% offering this material.

With respect to the contribution which computer and electronic materials make to supporting children's reading, multimedia CD-ROMs, computer software (excluding computer games) and Internet access are all seen as being very important. In terms of provision, however, multimedia CD-ROMs are available in almost three times as many respondents' departments (71%) as computer software. This is a most encouraging development, flagged up in Denham's research (1997), and an area of the collection that continues to expand. We are witnessing a slow growth in the provision of Internet access, with just over one third of responding authorities indicating that access is facilitated. Comments like the following from Stirling Libraries were evident in many of our interviews with library staff:

> *Access to a wide range of materials and library services is the key. Media, Internet access – in small communities the library is the centre of the community, which increases its visibility and value. An up-to-date collection . . . is essential.* (Stirling)

Over the past two years there is growing evidence that websites concerned with children's literature and reading are blossoming. For example, the section 'Threads from the web' in recent issues of *Youth Library Review* reveals a consistent stream of new sites, and the recent Stories on the Web initiative may act as a further stimulus to the Internet being used to support and encourage reading activity. Furthermore, authorities such as Knowsley and Derbyshire (DELTA networking) have established exciting new networking initiatives, which have been successful in attracting children and young adults. There was a strong sense that authorities perceived the need to foster development of Internet access, given that the requisite funding was made available through the government's commitment to developing the People's Network.

Another area that the study investigated was the value and provision of e-mail addresses. As yet little value is placed on this dimension of communication between children, and just over 5% of authorities facilitate such communication. There is anecdotal evidence from other countries, especially in the Far East and parts of Australia and North America, to suggest that children can improve their reading efficiency (and writing skills) through the use of e-mail. This is possibly an issue for consideration in the future.

The study did not reveal any significant differences in the coverage of these materials across library authorities in the UK, with the following exception: the English unitary authorities were above average in the provision of audiovisual materials.

Our study did not set out to explore the reasons underlying the slow development of electronic collections. However, the data gleaned from the case study interviews revealed one important common concern: the need to establish programmes covering a broad array of IT skills training. This concern echoes earlier research in this field (Lonsdale and Wheatley, 1990):

> *One problem is lack of staff expertise. There is a major need to train librarians in IT. Only three libraries have CD-ROMs for children, and we need to update our IT facilities generally. The Board paper is likely to include guidelines on purchase of hardware and software, and on competence levels. We have completed an audit of IT skills and will be acting on it.* (South Eastern Education and Library Board)

## Bibliographical sources and services

Writing in 1996, Elkin and Lonsdale made the following observation:

There exists in the UK . . . a large and diverse range of [bibliographical] sources although there has been little attempt to investigate the use made of these by children's librarians. (Elkin and Lonsdale, 1996, 146)

If collections are to give an accurate reflection of the reading needs of children, selection and evaluation must be undertaken in the most effective and efficient way. In part, success is dependent upon the quality of bibliographical sources and services, and their exploitation by library staff. Our study sought to address this issue, and we investigated the use made of bibliographical sources and services to support collection development.

Figure 4.1 indicates that a broad range of sources is used, but the data need to be viewed in the light of an initial question about the *importance* of each source. Of all of the sources in Figure 4.1, only library suppliers' approvals are both rated as important and used by a very high percentage of libraries. All other bibliographical sources were placed in the middle range in terms of their importance, contradicting the high degree of reported use.

Certainly, issues surrounding the use of approvals dominated our case studies. Many comments were made about the current issue of approvals collections being replaced by CD-ROMs, or about some of the responsibility for selection being devolved to library suppliers. Hampshire, amongst others, still perceived the importance of handling books in the selection of stock, not wishing to

*go down the same road as Hertfordshire which uses CD-ROMs.*

In arguing for the retention of the approvals, one library authority noted that the status and value of children's librarians stem in part from the very close relationship which they have with the bookstock. Powys libraries are indicative of another group

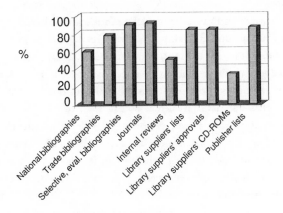

**Fig. 4.1**  *Libraries' use of selection materials*

of libraries, however, who see potential gains from using the CD-ROM in the selection process. SEELB noted that the quality of books in the approvals collections had dropped dramatically.

Another advantage of the approvals system relates to training and motivation of staff:

> We review all fiction before purchase, using Woodfield and a local bookseller, Cromwell, for an approval service. We're fighting to keep the appropriate system: it has a training and motivational element as well as being an effective way of selection. Hertfordshire is now using the Internet but our way means that the staff really know the books. We have selection meetings fortnightly, with a representative from each branch, where people present reviews and we then mark up the lists. The cost-effectiveness of the system is always being questioned, but we do see it as vital. We're about to trial a system of non-fiction subject approvals. (Croydon)

The high use of journals, such as *The School Librarian, Books for Keeps, Carousel* and *The Times Educational Supplement,* for selection is a manifestation of the comprehensive cover that they offer for children's *book* materials. Their coverage of *non-book* materials, and electronic resources in particular, is low compared with the output of publishing. The results of our study need to be interpreted with some care and there is a suggestion that the responses of librarians focused on the selection of book materials.

## The selection process

There has been some debate in the professional literature on the issue of the respective roles of professional and paraprofessional librarians participating in the selection of materials for children. Our data revealed that, whilst an unexpectedly high percentage of professional children's librarians (84%) took responsibility, 55% of staff were categorized as generalist professionals. Changes in management structures as a result of local government reorganization or internal modifications have led to some library authorities substituting skilled children's library personnel with generalists. Such changes raise important issues, the most prevalent being: do generalist staff possess the requisite knowledge and understanding of children's materials to engage fully in the development and exploitation of collections for children, their parents and carers?

Another issue that our data revealed was that 19% of paraprofessional staff participate in stock selection. The advantages of this – for example, the close affinity with the child user and his or her needs – is rehearsed elsewhere (Chapter 2). It would appear from this figure, and also from the comments gleaned in the case studies (in particular those made by paraprofessionals), that authorities do perceive the importance of exploiting their skills in this way.

Several authorities indicated their intention to develop a rapport between the public library and the education sector in the selection of material and in the development and promotion of the collection:

> *We're trying to build up a strategy of cooperation, and have just set up Telemeet, linking two branches and six schools to the Internet and CD-ROM network.* (Croydon)

## Interlibrary loans

For both terrestrial and virtual libraries, the issue of ensuring that the child can procure copies of material held outside its authority is of particular import. Our survey revealed that an encouraging 69% of authorities offer interlibrary loan facilities to young people. One divisional children's librarian exemplifies this progressive attitude towards facilitating access:

> *Children can request anything. They've got access to stock anywhere in the country, and access to children's librarians who are well-read and can guide them from one book to another and so help their reading development. Because of our stock selection system, we really do know the stock. One of the most important things is to give children access to the best of books, to sample and experiment.* (Hampshire)

## Access

Facilitating access to the collection, and ultimately to appropriate reading resources, is paramount, and we investigated the various means of access.

## Categorization

Critical to the successful exploitation of the collection is that its arrangement should accurately reflect the needs of the child and adult user rather than the perception that the librarian may have of the user's requirements. One approach to ensure that the children's collection satisfies the child's needs is to adopt a mode of categorization for the stock and to depart from the traditional concern with strict author or classification arrangement.

Our study explored the issue of how access impacts upon reading, and acquired considerable data on the nature of the categorization of children's and teenager's collections.

Ninety-nine percent of respondents placed picture books in a separate location. The existence of separate collections of picture books is long-standing, with many libraries designed specifically to accommodate this philosophy (Dewe, 1995).

What was particularly intriguing, however, was that 60% of these authorities undertook a further level of categorization. An analysis of how libraries grouped picture books is offered in Figure 4.2. The significance of age is important, reflecting a

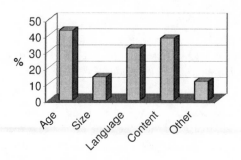

**Fig. 4.2**  *Categorization of picture books*

concern to distinguish levels and types of reading – an issue that was often stated in the policy statements – and reflecting the important growth in the publishing of picture books for the older readers. With respect to children's fiction, 93% of authorities used forms of categorization (see Figure 4.3).

The evidence in Figure 4.3 suggests strongly that librarians feel they can enhance access to fiction through the use of collections organized by age groups and reading ability. This is supported by evidence taken from the case studies:

> *We can help parents who would be intimidated going into school to ask what to get for their children. Grading of reading material is important, therefore, within libraries.* (Stirling)

There is, however, much less emphasis upon categorization by reading series, despite pronouncements in the professional literature that series fiction has played a particularly important role in helping to formulate choice. This is especially evident in the teenage library (Birmingham Libraries, 1994, 9).

Classification schemes still dominate in the categorization of non-fiction, and the low use of a broad subject approach is intriguing (see Figure 4.4). Several of the case study libraries intimated that categorization without a classification scheme was problematic for children and library staff when locating stock.

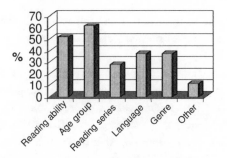

**Fig. 4.3**  *Categorization of fiction*

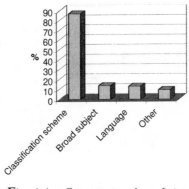

**Fig. 4.4**  *Categorization of non-fiction*

The division of children and teenage collections has long exercised the minds of librarians (Sharp, 1996, 37–41). Our study investigated the degree to which teenage material was separated from the children's collection and the forms in which it is housed. Ninety-nine percent of responding authorities provide specific teenage collections (see Figure 4.5).

The responses reveal a predilection towards housing teenage collections separately, and a slight bias towards locating them in proximity to the adult collection, mirroring the ambivalence within the professional literature on this subject. The case studies revealed that within the teenage collection, wherever it is housed, materials are usually categorized. The significance of Streetwise collections was reported, with authorities such as Northamptonshire actively encouraging teenagers to become involved in selecting and displaying the Streetwise stock. A range of other subdivisions was identified, corroborating evidence reported in other research studies (Sharp, 1996, 48–56). There was also an overwhelming consensus about the importance of face-on display in promoting the collection.

## Advantages of categorization

Such levels of categorization within children's libraries would suggest that libraries

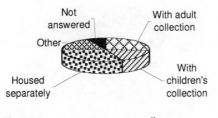

**Fig. 4.5**  *Location of teenage collection*

perceive substantial gains for children in terms of access and exploitation. Indeed, the scant literature on this subject does set out potential advantages for the child user (Hibbs et al, 1992; Elkin and Lonsdale, 1996, 154–5). Few librarians discussed their rationale for this, and the following extract constitutes a rare statement on this issue:

*The introduction of stock categorisation for children's fiction aims to increase the accessibility of the stock for children and young people . . .*

*The objectives of a countywide categorisation policy are outlined below:*

*i)   to increase the accessibility of stock;*
*ii)  to provide an introduction to library skills and adult stock categorisation;*
*iii) to promote positive presentation of stock;*
*iv)  to enable monitoring through statistical information, e.g. usage patterns, issues;*
*v)   to indicate popular areas of stock (promotion implications);*
*vi)  to provide some evidence of the development of reading habits.*

(Bedfordshire Libraries Stock Policy)

Paradoxically, only half of respondents indicated that they had evidence that categorization did benefit users. Of these, less than a quarter (20%) believe that categorization channels children to material of an appropriate reading level, and just less than one-third feel that it moves children to material of appropriate interest (see Figure 4.6).

For those libraries that do not categorize, or categorize to only a limited extent, the critical role that the librarian plays in guiding children and parents to appropriate reading resources was emphasized:

*We have general fiction categories but part of it is to say to staff that you can share and use a range of materials and part of the skill of developing a love of reading is that you experiment with different types of materials. We offer that range but we also offer support for parents and children in exper-*

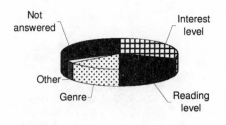

**Fig. 4.6**   *How categorization channels readers*

*imenting. We guide them to broad areas but we deliberately don't put age ranges or key stages on books. We don't want to compartmentalise things in that way but at the same time we understand how desperate some parents are to be guided and we know that whatever system we use is not adequate for everybody. What we are trying to do is not teach children to read but as they go through that reading process is support them at each stage . . . [and] we train staff to understand how children learn and how they can enjoy a range of reading styles or reading experiences. (Birmingham)*

Such guidance is at the heart of our professional remit and manifest in the professional guidelines on staffing (Blanshard, 1997). However, it should be recognized that in many authorities constraints exist. There were instances recorded by our researchers that the high level of suggested staff availability was not always the case:

*. . . the staff were not much involved in helping choose books at the shelves (they were too busy charging loans out). (Neath Port Talbot)*

The ambivalent attitudes that we discovered in the study towards the value of categorization seem to suggest a clear need for further investigations into the case for categorization.

## Information retrieval

Another critical factor in facilitating access and promoting the collection is the mode of information retrieval that is available to the user. Figure 4.7 sets out the range of approaches which are offered. The report *Investing in children* (LISC(E), 1995) applauded the growth of online public access catalogues (OPACs) in children's libraries. Our study revealed that a range of modes of information retrieval were used and that almost one-third of children's libraries who responded still did not have an OPAC (see Fig-

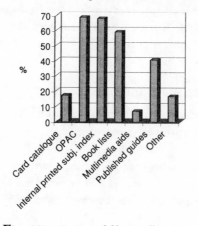

**Fig. 4.7**  *Access to children's collections*

ure 4.7). A number of the libraries that participated in the case studies did indicate their intention of developing OPACs in the near future, and undoubtedly this is a prevalent trend.

Whilst there were no discernible issues common to all libraries, some concerns did surface. Several librarians intimated that there would be real advantage to having networked links between the OPACs in the public libraries and those in nearby schools. The projected development of the People's Network may well facilitate such provision.

Another issue was the need for more training packages for young people to learn about accessing the OPAC, and there were several authorities that felt that more pertinent interfaces similar to the KidsCatalog should be developed to enhance the process of searching.

Figure 4.7 reveals that there is a strong reliance upon the use of internal printed subject indexes and, to a lesser extent, upon published guides to the collection. Book lists, too, are still highly regarded, and many of the librarians indicated that these comprised recommendations taken from children.

The scant use of multimedia aids such as Bookwizard is intriguing. Several years ago, when the Bookwizard multimedia programme was launched, there appeared to be a future for an information device that offered such an innovative and attractive interface for children (Lonsdale, 1994, 1996). It would be interesting to explore further why such multimedia aids have not developed more widely in children's libraries.

## Book reviewing

Several authorities emphasized the success they had in using book reviews from children to enhance access to the collection and to relevant reading material:

> Book reviewing was introduced recently to develop a system as a better basis of giving advice and recommending good reads across the range of reading materials. For National Libraries Week we have got a group of high school children to review books for each other. That will be really good, because it is so much harder to reach teenagers. (Leeds)

## Management issues surrounding access

Few authorities discussed the management issues surrounding access to the collection. One paraprofessional librarian suggested:

> . . . periodically rearranging the stock, in the same way supermarkets periodically rearrange their shelves, to make the public more aware of what is available by forcing them to pay more attention to where they are looking, bringing new things to their attention. (Ynys Môn)

Several libraries raised the issue of physical access to materials, indicating that there were still problems associated with inaccessible and 'intimidating' shelving, especially for the younger child. In one library our researcher observed the following:

> *The OPAC is not working, but some children use the subject guide. Unfortunately this is way above the children's eye-level, so not everyone can read it easily and the smaller children are particularly disadvantaged.* (Leeds)

## Children's views

Children's views of access were often intriguing and bring out some of the more fundamental issues which we face daily. In answer to the question: Do you usually find what you are looking for? one child said:

> *Yes and no; there are not enough copies of titles and too often books are out on loan or missing.*

Another child said he couldn't find books because they were

> *squashed together on the shelves.* (Ynys Môn)

## Conclusions

During the preparation of this chapter a literature search was undertaken to ascertain existing documentation on the subject. Over the past two decades there has been a dearth of writing about the synergy that exists between collection development and the provision of materials to support reading in children's libraries. Our study offers a small corrective, providing new insights into the nature of collection development.

Whilst the value of having a comprehensive written policy for collection development is recognized by the children's library profession in the UK, many of the comparatively small number of written statements made available to us do not go beyond a statement of selection and acquisition to embrace collection evaluation and review and promotion.

Perhaps more importantly, in the context of this study, children's libraries do need to set out more extensive statements about how they see collection development supporting their institution's aims regarding the promotion of literacy in all its manifestations. Greater delineation, perhaps, is required of the library's precise definition of literacy.

Although children's librarians do consult a broad array of bibliographical sources and services for selection, acquisition and evaluation, the critical contribution that library suppliers' approvals collections make in helping staff to select titles relevant to children's reading needs and interests is highlighted in our consideration of the bibliographical apparatus used to support collection development. However, our study revealed concerns about the potential demise of this service.

Categorization of the collection is employed widely through children's and teenage libraries, with a variety of methods being used. It is paradoxical that librarians feel ambivalent about the role of categorization in helping the child to connect with appropriate reading and viewing material, thereby enhancing literacy.

There is general agreement that access in its many manifestations is critical in helping children engage with appropriate books and non-book material, and our study suggests that we are on the threshold of widespread OPAC development.

The research raised many questions that now require further investigation. To what extent have changes in the management structure of children's libraries impacted upon the devolution of responsibility for selection, evaluation and acquisition? If the new literacies are to be supported, do children's librarians yet possess the requisite evaluation skills and acquisition knowledge to identify and exploit electronic resources? Such questions ensure that investigations will continue.

## References

Barton, D (1994) *Literacy: an introduction to the ecology of written language*, Blackwell.

Birmingham Libraries (1994) *Teenagers, books and libraries: a report into the way young people use libraries and choose books*, Birmingham Library Services.

Blanshard, C (ed) (1997) *Children and young people: Library Association guidelines for public library services*, 2nd edn, Library Association Publishing.

Denham, D (1997) Children and IT in public libraries: a research project, *Youth Library Review*, **23**, (Spring), 20–9.

Dewe, M (1995) *Planning and designing libraries for children and young people*, Library Association Publishing.

Elkin, J and Lonsdale, R (eds) (1996) *Focus on the child: libraries, literacy and learning*, Library Association Publishing.

Glancy, K (1982) Kids and comics, *Bookmark*, **9**, 11.

Hibbs, E et al (1992) The case for categorisation: an investigation of children's selection methods, *Youth Library Review*, **14**, (Autumn), 16–19.

Library and Information Services Council (England) Working Party on Library Services for Children and Young People (1995) *Investing in children: the future of library services for children and young people*, Library Information Series 22, HMSO.

Library Association (1991) *Children and young people: Library Association guidelines for public library services*, Library Association Publishing.

Lonsdale, R (1994) Enter the Bookwizard, *Youth Library Review*, **18**, (Autumn), 5–13.

Lonsdale, R (1996) Information technology and the promotion of children's reading, *Hong Kong Library Association Journal*, **18**, 119–25.

Lonsdale, R and Everitt, J (1996) Breaking down the barriers: the provision of modern foreign language material to young people in public libraries in the UK, *Journal of Librarianship and Information Science*, **28** (2), 71–81.

Lonsdale, R and Wheatley, A (1990) *Provision of audiovisual and computer materials to young people by British public libraries*, BNB Research Fund 49, The British Library.

Moon, C (1977) Comic comments: constructive uses of comic techniques, *Junior Education*, (1 May), 27.

Sharp, D S (1996) *The examination of public library provision and promotion for teenagers, with particular reference to the United States and Great Britain* (unpublished MSc dissertation), Department of Information and Library Studies, University of Wales Aberystwyth.

CHAPTER 5

# Promotion

Debbie Denham

> Storytelling is probably the most under-rated and best activity
> we organise (Hampshire)

## Introduction

This chapter focuses specifically on library promotion, which is concerned with the development and support of children's reading. It looks at promotional activities and how valuable they were perceived to be, looking in detail at examples of book-based activities. The role of knowledgeable children's librarians supporting children's reading development, and the need for both recognition and training to be part of the library's strategy, are considered. Management issues, including evaluation and monitoring, are also addressed, alongside key local partnerships and national initiatives.

## Promotion

Promotion takes many forms within children's library services. It can take the form of:

- the library building and vehicles
- staff
- contact with groups
- events and activities
- displays and exhibitions
- publicity.

Methods of promotion have evolved over time and are subject to constant reappraisal and shifting focus. This changing emphasis is discussed later in the chapter, but is here centred on books and reading. Children's librarians have long been involved in promotion:

> The use of promotional tools by library services is very wide and has often been particularly focused on children's services. (Kinnell, 1996, 170)

Kinnell questions, however, whether promotional expertise and activity has been placed within a strategic marketing framework. The importance of implementing a coordinated marketing strategy was raised in Chapter 3 where it was linked to the identification and targeting of specific clients. The literature reminds us here that one of the particular features affecting the promotion of children's library services is the variety of target audiences:

- children of all ages and intellectual and physical abilities and from a wide range of cultural backgrounds
- parents and other carers
- teachers
- governing bodies
- staff
- elected members
- the profession. (Blanshard, 1997, 54)

Eyre supports the vital place which promotion has in children's service development. She identifies the need for promotional activity to be more clearly defined and targeted, particularly during times of financial constraint:

> Ironically, in times of constrained resources, funding for effective PR [public relations] and promotion is often given low status and is one of the first areas to be cut. Yet it is arguably even more essential that the value and role of libraries of all kinds are communicated effectively to actual and potential users, those who have control of budgets and politicians at all levels. (Eyre, 1996, 174)

How might we define what promotion means? Eyre suggests that promotion:

> . . . may be described as the gaining of public support for an activity, cause, movement or institution . . . a planned continuous communication effort designed to gain support by developing mutual understanding and co-operation between an organisation and its publics. (Eyre, 1996, 178)

De Saez highlights some of the confusion between marketing and promotion and indicates that:

> . . . marketing communication is a better description than is 'promotion' of the activities involved . . . Communication is one of the things which librarians and information professionals tend to be very good at. (De Saez, 1993)

Definitions vary but all suggest that promotion and communication of the range of services and facilities in libraries are an important element of service provision:

> Promotion is a vital part of service delivery and is not something to be 'added on' . . . Promotion to children should be an integral part of the strategies for promoting the whole service. (Blanshard, 1997, 53)

Promotional activities often operate within the internal environment of the library. This, though, is potentially limiting as the purpose is to reach non-users, too:

> There is growing recognition that the library is not a building. It may be based within a building but services, facilities and functions extend beyond these confines and will necessitate undertaking promotional activities in the wider community . . . working in the community ensures that non-users of the library are targeted and they are arguably more important in terms of promotional activities than the children and adults who use the library service as a matter of course. (Eyre, 1994, 14–15)

> Knowledge is power. Access to that knowledge can provide a foundation-stone for life. As children are at the beginning of life, they have the right to know what is available to them, either directly or through the adults who care for them, whether parent or teacher. (Eyre, 1996, 179)

People may be non-users for a variety of reasons, but if social inclusion is part of the library's remit, then an awareness of the library's services should be the right of all. It is vital for all children, parents and carers to know that the library is there for them. Eyre reminds us:

> The power of libraries is available only to those with access to and knowledge of all those facilities offered by a good library . . . Promotion may offer everyone a lifetime library and information entitlement, a right to our highest quality of service, through improved diffusion and our best practice across all organisational sectors . . . promotion . . . must begin with the rights and needs of children. (Eyre, 1996, 178–9)

## Supporting reading

The primary role of the public library of encouraging the development of children's reading and love of books has been continually reiterated in a series of reports, including: *Borrowed time?: the future of public libraries in the UK* (Comedia, 1993), *Review of the public library service in England and Wales* (Aslib, 1995) and *Investing in children: the future of library services for children and young people* (LISC(E), 1995). One of the core purposes of the public library was identified in the Aslib Review as:

> . . . to enlighten children, by enabling and encouraging them to discover information and the advantages of reading. (Aslib, 1995, 12)

This perspective was vociferously maintained in the report's survey of both the general public and library staff alike and reinforced in *Investing in children*:

> One of the critical factors in the encouragement of reading among children and young people is that books should be both available and accessible: available in the sense of being in places where children can get at them, accessible in the sense that any child, either independently or through intermediary help and guidance, can use them.

> By making books available to all who want them, together with specialist staff to make them accessible through advice and assistance in the choice and use of them, libraries are uniquely placed to make a significant contribution to the encouragement of reading among children and young people. (LISC(E), 1995, 15–16)

The role of libraries and promotion of reading in cultural enrichment was highlighted in *Borrowed time?*:

> Providing a choice of books, recorded music, videos across a range of interests; acting as an entry point for children into literacy and 'the book of life', storytelling, after-school activities, offering a home to art exhibitions, talks and debates, poetry-readings, and various forms of literature promotion.

> The library space is regarded as a sanctuary, a place where one may sit, read, browse, sleep, and remain unharrassed; nobody is judged and therefore nobody is found wanting. (Comedia, 1993, 17)

Such a positive attitude held by the general public towards library services is a key selling point and promotional opportunity for libraries. In MORI polls, libraries are regularly voted the most popular local government service and seen as a service which provides considerable value for money.

A knowledge and understanding of what is being promoted and an enthusiasm for it, underpins all successful PR and promotion. (Eyre, 1994, 7)

## Promotion of children's reading

The nationwide survey conducted for A Place for Children included questions specific to this chapter and designed to identify:

- the value placed on promotion by library authorities
- the potential contribution of a range of promotional activities for supporting children's reading
- the use and value of a variety of promotional tools, eg Teletext, web home pages
- the availability and uptake of partnership and funding opportunities
- library support for specific reading-focused activities, eg family reading groups, homework initiatives.

The library service has a portfolio of products which it needs to promote effectively. The traditional well-defined areas of resource and service provision are only part of the picture. There are some intangible elements which libraries need to promote. Libraries have provided a free lending service for so long that there is an ingrained belief that everyone must be aware of this fact. However, particularly in the light of societal changes and the move to a more commercially based culture, libraries can be seen as an anachronism; as one student teacher noted:

*It is outmoded because it is free. Libraries need to promote the idea of this asset so people don't take it for granted.*

The results in terms of evidence of strategic planning of promotional activity were rather disappointing. Only 24% of library authorities had a general authority-wide marketing strategy for library services, although 27% indicated that they had specific promotional policies for the children's and teenagers' library service, 50% of which were part of the overall library marketing policy. This would suggest that in some authorities the children's librarians had developed independent strategies to inform their promotional activities planning and implementation. The need for and value of strategic planning is evident in the literature:

Strategies are the day-to-day reason for being here and formalising them in writing enables you to justify the reason for the service, its impact and coverage . . . Setting strategies for a service involves a consistent process of planning and action, based upon reality and focused on success. (Blanshard, 1998, 89)

By the 1960s children's services were highly developed, if piecemeal, and included a range of services to teenagers. Developments since then show no evidence, though, of a coherent, strategic approach to children's library work, in line with theories of strategic management and marketing. (Kinnell, 1996, 162)

## Promotional activities

The questionnaire survey sought to rate the potential contribution of individual promotional activities to the promotion process. Printed publicity was felt to be the most effective means of promoting the library service in all authority types (84%). The least effective and least used was Teletext, although this may be explained by its relative obsolescence and the fact that Teletext has been superseded by the relatively cheap method of using web pages as a means of promoting libraries. Responses indicated that children's library web pages were not yet widely available (ie in only 26% of authorities) but that their value was relatively highly rated by those authorities which did provide them. This appears to support the current general lack of awareness of the potential of IT as indicated in the survey and reinforced by earlier research. (Denham et al, 1996; Denham, 1997)

Traditional methods of promotion such as using printed material are still widely used, but it is evident that IT is starting to be recognized as a possible way forward. The use of IT, particularly in the development of web pages, has considerable advantages over print-based methods. It has the potential to reach larger numbers of children relatively cheaply and to make that contact outside the library environment as well as within. Internet connections also provide the potential of opening up communication channels via e-mail (see also Chapter 4). Local newspapers were used by a large proportion of authorities (70%), as has been recognized by Eyre:

Using the media has obvious advantages for public relations and promotion as it is possible to get a message across to a wider audience. One of the most common uses of media is through local radio and newspapers. (Eyre, 1994, 22)

Table 5.1 demonstrates the average rating attached to each activity on a scale of 0–5 and the percentage of authorities who use these promotional tools. This demonstrates that those authorities which did not employ a specific promotional tool rated them less highly than those authorities which did.

The use of printed promotional literature, and the practice of using schools as a vehicle of service promotion to children, is widespread.

The commitment of children's librarians to children's reading is demonstrated by the considerable range of promotional activities offered both internally and outside the library. The relative benefits of these activities is difficult to determine, although, as Blanshard noted:

Most library activities will in some way foster literacy, or provide a model for parents to emulate. Storytelling, or simply sharing stories together, is not only enjoyable for children, but enables the library service to prompt parents to make time for this activity themselves. Reading games, holiday events and other promotions can provide assistance with literacy. (Blanshard, 1997, 22)

Respondents were asked to rate the importance of activities for their potential contribution to the promotion of children's and teenagers' reading as demonstrated in Table 5.2. Visits from institutions were perceived as vitally important in supporting children's reading. These visits provide local schools and under-fives groups with the opportunity of visiting the library to borrow books, to take part in storytelling and library orientation sessions, and to make use of library staff expertise when selecting materials. Reaching children through under-fives groups and schools provides the library with a 'captive audience' of prospective readers and library users. Developing relationships with schools ensures that libraries can reach the majority of 5–16-year-olds in the UK. As well as reaching children, institutional visits to the library also provide an opportunity to reach and educate parents, teachers and carers. The importance of other book-based activities, including author readings, storytelling and reading games, was also acknowledged in the questionnaire survey.

Janet Hill (1973) expressed her belief in the importance of librarians working within the local community, often outside the library building. Twenty-five years later A Place for Children demonstrates the importance attached to activities delivered outside the library (see Table 5.3). Book-based activities were prominent, while promotion of books by storytelling and talking to parents and carers was also seen as important. The tangible provision of books through book boxes and bulk loans was also viewed as significant. The key facets which underpinned activities in libraries were: getting books into the hands of children and those concerned with their reading; and promoting the importance of reading and books to parents, teachers and other professionals.

**Table 5.1**  *Average importance ratings by provision of activities, UK as a whole*

|  | Teletext | Videos | CD-ROM | Web home page | Local paper | Local radio | Printed publicity |
|---|---|---|---|---|---|---|---|
| Authorities which provide | 2.6 | 3.7 | 4.3 | 3.8 | 4.0 | 3.9 | 4.3 |
| Authorities which do not provide | 2.6 | 3.2 | 3.5 | 3.4 | 3.8 | 3.4 | 4.1 |
| % of authorities providing | 8 | 42 | 42 | 26 | 70 | 38 | 84 |

**Table 5.2**  *Average importance ratings by provision of activities, UK as a whole*

|  | Authorities which provide | Authorities which do not provide | % of authorities providing |
|---|---|---|---|
| Visits from institutions | 4.7 | 5.0 | 98 |
| IT provision/support | 4.4 | 3.8 | 57 |
| Storytelling | 4.6 | 3.9 | 90 |
| Holiday activities | 4.4 | 3.6 | 95 |
| Author readings | 4.3 | 3.3 | 88 |
| Parent meetings | 4.0 | 3.2 | 19 |
| Reading groups | 4.1 | 3.6 | 27 |
| Homework clubs | 4.3 | 3.9 | 27 |
| Reading games | 4.2 | 3.0 | 50 |
| User groups | 4.5 | 3.3 | 22 |
| Venue for clubs | 3.6 | 2.7 | 4 |
| Parent and child facilities | 3.9 | 3.4 | 36 |
| Language user groups | 4.1 | 3.1 | 17 |
| Library tours | 3.9 | 3.2 | 66 |
| Book quizzes | 3.8 | 3.0 | 73 |
| Exhibitions | 3.8 | 2.9 | 84 |
| Visiting drama/music | 3.9 | 2.9 | 60 |
| Joining packs | 4.3 | 4.1 | 49 |
| Reading lists | 4.1 | 3.8 | 69 |
| Bookmarks/leaflets | 3.9 | 3.3 | 84 |
| Library newsletter | 3.7 | 3.1 | 14 |
| Signposting | 4.5 | 3.7 | 86 |
| Information shop | 4.0 | 3.2 | 10 |
| Information skills programme | 4.5 | 3.7 | 60 |
| Educating carers | 4.6 | 3.8 | 64 |

In the case study interviews, questions relating to promotion identified:

- the importance attached to the promotion of children's reading as indicated by service priorities and objectives
- whether promotional activity was targeted and if so at whom
- the effectiveness and significance of the library in promoting children's reading
- partnerships and cooperation in the promotion of children's reading, eg within the local authority, between library authorities

- any relationships between children's and adult's reading promotion
- the range and uptake of promotional activities
- evaluation strategies for promotional activities
- the availability and nature of training and training needs in the promotion of children's reading
- perceived gaps in the promotion of children's reading.

## General promotion

Despite cutbacks, the importance of promotion as a central activity in service delivery to children and young people was being maintained:

*The whole service revolves around promotion, including stock arrangement.*

although it was still acknowledged that:

*A lot of what we have done is ad hoc.*

Some library authorities had made considerable advances in marketing services and resources, and there were examples of marketing officers being employed directly by libraries to very good effect, as one teacher acknowledged:

*The library is becoming more effective at promotion, it wasn't very good in the past, there was a lack of funding. Libraries weren't highlighted in the media or at school. Libraries have become more interesting places to go to.*

**Table 5.3**  *Average importance ratings by provision of activities, UK as a whole*

| | Visits to insti-tutions | Story-telling | Holiday activity | Bulk loans | Book boxes | Book buses | Book quizzes | Walks | Exhib-itions | Co-operative ventures | Edu-cating minders |
|---|---|---|---|---|---|---|---|---|---|---|---|
| Authorities which provide | 4.5 | 4.1 | 4.1 | 4.4 | 4.3 | 4.3 | 3.9 | 3.5 | 3.8 | 4.3 | 4.5 |
| Authorities which do not provide | 3.8 | 3.5 | 3.1 | 3.5 | 3.5 | 3.6 | 3.2 | 2.1 | 3.2 | 3.4 | 3.6 |
| % of authorities providing | 90 | 36 | 57 | 64 | 39 | 21 | 37 | 6 | 59 | 30 | 70 |

A parent suggested:

> *Libraries do a lot more than they did in the past and are better at asking their customers' opinions of the service.*

In one authority a national initiative had proved to be the stimulus for the development of a strategic approach:

> *As The Year of Reading approaches, we shall be looking at a strategic approach.*

Despite an apparent reluctance on the part of many library authorities wholeheartedly to embrace strategic approaches to promotion and marketing, the case studies provided evidence suggesting a considerable need for this. It is of great concern that interested, concerned parents and members of the general public are still not even aware of where libraries are geographically situated within their local communities:

> *I didn't know there was a library here for the first four years I lived here.*

Promotion evidently needs to start at a very basic level:

> *Sometimes we are not very good at saying things which are very obvious to us. Sometimes we need to be a bit more open to say 'You don't have to pay to borrow books.' At one point we assumed that everyone knew libraries are free but our research very clearly showed us that parents did not know.*

It is not enough to promote services and resources within a library environment when people are unaware of the library's existence. The problem of preaching to the converted was raised in a number of authorities:

> *Attracting new readers is vital.*

> *The people who do not join their children in this area are the ones who are scared of libraries and you really need to promote libraries to the parents there.*

## Promoting reading

Staff, parents and teachers interviewed all recognized the prime importance of libraries in providing a wide range of books and other materials. Access to these materials, and the nurturing role of knowledgeable librarians in fostering a love of reading, were also seen as vital to the development of the growing child. Many children's librarians felt they were best serving the needs of the child and its parents by:

*. . . providing the widest possible range of good children's literature; by promoting reading and libraries.*

These findings were reinforced by staff at all levels as well as by parents and teachers:

*One of the essential parts of what we do is to encourage children to read and through promotions and various activities to keep them reading.*

*. . . to promote reading, to make children aware of the potential in books for enjoyment, information and education.*

The strength of the library service was perceived as the promotion of reading for pleasure as opposed to the pedagogy of reading undertaken by schools. This distinction was articulated as the engendering of a love of reading and books rather than the development of specific reading skills. The latter was generally seen as the exclusive remit of schools and teachers, although there are clearly misconceptions about what literacy means (see Chapter 2):

*. . . we promote good quality children's literature. That encourages them to read books, but it is not about the reading skill.*

*Reading is promoted but literacy is not, this is seen as the job of the schools.*

*What we are trying to develop, what we are trying to do is not teach children to read but as they go through that reading process is support them at each stage.*

The fun role of libraries in promoting reading and literature, as opposed to the educational role of teaching and developing specific skills, was continually reiterated:

*The message that reading is not just about reading scheme performance, but something they can do for fun.*

This focus on enjoyment, however, should not diminish the importance of the library's role in supporting the development of children's reading. This was clearly expressed by one respondent, who was deeply concerned that libraries should not be seen merely as supporters of leisure reading. The negative connotations which could be attached to terms such as fun and enjoyment could serve to undermine the importance of what libraries do. The library is absolutely fundamental to the child developing reading skills:

*I don't think we have done enough to promote the power of our reading. It's not just nice leisure reading, it's reading that's essential.*

Teachers, parents and library staff all recognized the importance of libraries in supporting this broader definition of reading, and the value of librarians modelling good reading behaviours was summed up by one teacher:

> It is important that children see everybody reading and get to know a range of books. It is impossible to have everything at school and some children don't have any books at home at all, so libraries are good for the wide range. Reading outside school is very important so that children can see that people carry on reading even if they don't have to. Reading for fun is very important, and libraries are probably better at promoting that than schools are. (Leeds)

As part of their role, library staff, parents and teachers saw it as vital that a wide range of materials complementary to those provided in school should be made available by public libraries.

## Parents and families

Libraries have long worked with parents to support children's reading, and there was a clearly expressed need to continue this relationship:

> We could do more to encourage parents – often they're not sure where to look for books for their child.

The questionnaire survey identified that much of the promotion of reading was now taking a stronger family focus. Libraries had a strong role in supporting families, family reading and family visits to the library. The library was an environment which could meet the needs of all the family at the same time. All family members might find services tailored to their individual needs as long as they were made aware of what was available:

> Children's librarians . . . will speak to groups of parents, will talk to parents, will talk about storytelling with parents, give them hints and will deal with the enquiries that come from parents' own literacy difficulties.

> More take-up from parents since the class visits.

Family literacy was another trend, simultaneously supporting adult and child literacy skills development. The relationship between poor levels of literacy amongst parents and poor childhood literacy and reading development was acknowledged by a number of respondents. The emphasis on family-based cooperation was stressed and demonstrated by the number of authorities involved in or contemplating family reading groups.

## Book-based activities

The provision of activities has long been considered as a significant element of children's library service provision. The survey demonstrated clearly that this continued to be seen as a fundamental role of the library service throughout public libraries. The majority of children's libraries organized some form of 'activities' – an umbrella term for the resource-based promotional events held within the library and in the community. They were seen as an essential, important and integral part of library services to young people. The term covered planned events organized either by library staff alone or in cooperation with other groups. Activities were a means of encouraging children to become active borrowers, thereby increasing issues. They were also a vital means of attracting children who might make use of library resources and services although not becoming full members. The power of these programmes to attract large numbers of children was evidenced, for example, in Leeds Libraries' Summer Reading Scheme in 1997, which attracted 9000 children.

There has, however, been an evident shift in emphasis following a reassessment and refocusing on the role of the children's librarian in recent years. The case studies and the questionnaire survey both identified a move towards book-based promotion – a reaffirmation of books as the fundamental pivot around which library provision revolves. This was in contrast to the days when events were not necessarily directly related to reading or information. The reason for this was articulated as the need to move away from competing with other agencies which could provide purely entertainment-focused events, possibly more effectively than libraries:

*We have pulled back from the 'mini-entertainment' venue.*

*The summer reading game this year was very book based in response to staff criticism of previous summer promotions.*

This had often been motivated by criticisms from both staff and parents:

*. . . too much emphasis on colour-ins and mask-making . . . getting children into the library is different from getting them to read. I strongly feel that libraries should drop the daft activities and focus on promoting reading by storytelling, etc.*

Despite the evident support for this refocusing, some concern was expressed by front-line library staff about the wisdom of this approach:

*Everything is built around stories, reading or information books . . . everything is routed back into the reading issue. We found from our statistics that the staff in community libraries were worried that if they didn't have something like that [activities] children would not come. That has not proved the case at all but it felt like a step in the dark for some people to rely on the numbers coming in.*

Some of this concern was a result of the pressure to quantify all levels of service provision, to provide statistics which indicated high numbers of children attending events. Staff were worried about falling book issues and attendance at events, because that was still seen as a major measure of success. It required careful consideration to juxtapose the need to increase issues with the importance of maintaining the credibility of the library service. Libraries needed to be seen to provide activities which supported their core purposes. Summer reading programmes employed a considerable proportion of library promotional budgets, in terms of finance and staff time. Reading activities were seen as an important contribution to the library service in a number of ways:

*Storytelling is probably the most underrated and best activity we organise.* (Hampshire)

*The whole point about the summer reading promotion is that it keeps children reading for those six weeks and . . . if they don't practise those skills and they don't keep reading, then they go back to school in September and they've fallen behind.* (Northamptonshire)

There was some concern that libraries need to both sustain the effects of promotion and meet the demand thus stimulated, illustrating the need for this process to be proactive and planned, fitting into previously defined objectives, rather than reactive or based on previous practice alone.

Authorities used a variety of techniques to manage promotional activities. One authority allowed and encouraged individual community libraries to opt into authority-wide promotional programmes such as reading trails. This ensured that within the individual local library there was sufficient staff support for, and commitment to, the activity to ensure its success. The disadvantage of this approach was that it relied on staff commitment to the ideology of promotion and its value to children. This could therefore disadvantage certain children within the community if individual libraries consistently 'opt out' of authority-wide events.

## Sponsorship and external partnerships

Much of the sponsorship which took place in libraries was used for the delivery of promotional activities. Books and reading were prime worthy causes, demonstrated by the recent Royal Mail sponsorship deal for the Carnegie and Greenaway Awards, and by initiatives such as the Andrex Storytime, of which Northamptonshire was a pilot authority. Other sponsorship deals focused on local commerce, such as Sainsbury's.

Maintaining a commitment to funding projects was seen as problematic. It was often possible to access funding for the development of new initiatives, but difficult to maintain this after the initial period had elapsed. It is clearly vital that projects should be sustainable and that commercial sponsors should not have the power to affect the long-term running of projects. This short-termism in funding projects for one year and then consigning them to the scrap heap is a particular concern in many authorities.

## The book trade

Publishers and booksellers have long been partners of libraries:

> *In the Spring and Autumn we have fortnightly author visits . . . [I see] that programme is funded by publishers.*

This was indicative of the hard work which librarians in the children's sector have put into developing and maintaining links with publishers. A clear definition of the relationship was seen as necessary to justify the differences and inherent similarities between the two organizations.

> *I don't see us as competing with bookshops . . . [I see] bookshops as partners in promoting the book.*

## Knowledgeable librarians

Fundamental to this support for reading development was the important role given to librarians as central to the process; the need for librarians to be active rather than passive was also asserted. This was reinforced by parents:

> *The library is good at promoting reading particularly because of its friendly staff.*

by librarians:

> *A pro-active role in encouraging reading.*

> *Libraries have to be proactive in the field, 'it is up to us to be in there'.*

and by teachers:

> *People promote books, and the librarians are very knowledgeable. They're able to introduce books, spread enthusiasm, give you something you can take back to your class.* (Hampshire)

Words which respondents continually used in reference to children's librarians and their role in reading promotion were:

* confidence
* encouragement
* fun.

The role of the children's librarian was seen as:

- personally linking children and books
- promoting and encouraging a love of reading
- encouraging favourable attitudes to reading
- associating books with enjoyment as a priority
- promoting the enjoyment of reading.

To support children's reading, children's library staff needed to have an in-depth knowledge of the materials available. When lists were drawn up specifying the required skills for children's librarians, the following, relating specifically to reading development, tended to be emphasized over and over again:

- a detailed knowledge of children's books, IT hardware and software, AV multi-media etc
- a knowledge of appropriate information resources and an ability to assess them
- storytelling and other performance skills
- teaching skills to promote effective library use
- promotional skills, particularly with regard to book promotion.

Children's librarians were seen as constantly matching the child to the book. They were usually the only person with this particular expertise, this particular subject knowledge, providing the right material for the individual child:

> Small children choose much more freely than older children, so we attract the under fives to give children as much choice as possible at an early age. Older children often tend to narrow their range, for example to the Goosebumps series, and then it is harder to encourage them to read more widely. (Leeds)

Teachers and parents were seen to be largely unaware of the full range of books available to support reading for pleasure, and parents were often daunted by the vast numbers of books available in bookshops and libraries. The desire to provide materials for the individual child was tempered with the need also to respond to the requests of adults including teachers and parents. In practice this meant that librarians needed to provide:

> . . . some of what they want as well as what adults think they should have.

Library staff needed to be confident enough to provide guidance and encouragement to children, parents and carers, teachers and other professionals working with children:

*All our staff in their service plans make a commitment to serving children.*

In some cases this included paraprofessionals as well as qualified librarians or children's specialists, who were allowed to organize and take part in promotional activities.

When interviewed, however, some paraprofessionals indicated that they felt their skills were not recognized or utilized as much as they could be:

*We get the occasional school visit, but only professional staff get involved in these, even if they are plainly uncomfortable with children. To me it would make more sense to involve staff that are good with children, whether they are professional or not.*

One library manager identified a concern about the wastage of skills if staff were not able to achieve their full potential because of rigid demarcation of tasks:

*Staff are the most underused resource in terms of promotion . . . It is important to develop individuals and give them creative responsibility.*

Today's children have become more sophisticated and are exposed to a more sophisticated range of media in terms of content and presentation. Books, reading and libraries need to compete with these on an equal footing. The benefits of this were evident to library staff:

*It is great to see the children getting involved and to see we are offering a real alternative to TV and computers.*

The recent renewal of interest in adult literature promotion through public libraries owes much to the energies and expertise of children's librarians. Children's librarians are readily accepted as experts in fiction promotion and reader development, and the need to use this resource in adult reader development was articulated by two respondents:

*Children's Services have led the way in the promotion of reading and it does have a key, active role.*

*. . . we know and understand that actually children's librarians are streets ahead in terms of effective activities management. You really are rather silly if you try and reinvent the wheel rather than go to the experts, your children's librarians.* (Leeds)

## Training and education

In the case study, authorities staff expressed the need for more training in all aspects of promotional activities, including display. This was compounded by the belief that newly qualified graduates rarely studied specialized modules which equipped them for promotional work and working with children. Particular gaps in LIS education were identified in the questionnaire survey as: the role and practical implementation of promotional activities, a lack of knowledge of marketing and promotional techniques, and a lack of knowledge about how to promote literature. One authority indicated a concern that new professionals have little awareness of how to promote their own professionalism. There was evidence of concern that newly qualified practitioners should have not only a theoretical knowledge of children and child development, but also some practical experience in marketing, promotion and the management of activity programmes. This dichotomy between the practical and the theoretical continues to find an echo in the arguments around professional education and the need for graduates who have not only an increasing portfolio of skills but also a degree of specialist knowledge and experience. The lack of training in monitoring and evaluation was also mentioned, and this has direct repercussions when considered next to the low level and rather superficial quality of much of the evaluation which is undertaken of promotional events (this is discussed later in this chapter).

The continuing debate in professional education about the need for specialist and/or generalist staff was particularly pertinent in relation to the vital role which the children's librarian has in promoting reading:

*A generalist approach cuts staff off from specialist knowledge of books and clients.*

Many specialist children's librarians still felt they had gaps in their knowledge, and in particular a  need for more display training in connection with children's reading and how to encourage teenagers to read more widely. Staff indicated that their skills were often obtained through experience on the job rather than through specific training:

*I learn through author visits, visits to other libraries and membership of the children's book panel.*

The overwhelming demand from all levels of staff working in children's libraries was for time in which to keep up-to-date in the field, particularly with children's literature. The need for knowledge of new and innovative ways of promoting reading and literacy was constantly called for by professional librarians. Sharing of expertise across authorities, and awareness of good practice in other authorities, were felt to be vital for service improvement. Some authorities had invested heavily in staff training and ran courses including elements such as: customer care, equality issues, the library service's relationship with education, the library's role in education, and support for the family. Although the importance of up-dating was acknowledged, it was not always easy for this to be achieved:

*Difficult to keep in touch with national issues and what is going on and my personal reading for work.*

Although nearly all library authorities (97%) acknowledged the benefits of training in promotion, only 63% actually offered it. Similar figures were also found in the area of training for activities: 90% of authorities perceived it as beneficial, with only 50% actually offering it. Counties and London authorities provided the most positive picture as regards training of staff in promotion. At the time of the survey, newly formed unitary authorities had not had the time or the budgets to implement adequate training packages.

## A child-friendly environment

The public library provides an informal space within which the promotion of reading can take place. The provision of an inviting and appropriate library environment was noted as highly significant by library staff:

> We do a lot to support reading indirectly and that is just as important as any particular initiative. We ensure that there is a child friendly environment, for example, and try to overcome problems with listed buildings and staff attitude . . . also we make sure that the stock is appropriate and that materials are generally accessible, and that, for example, the shelves are not too high. (Leeds)

> This is a warm safe place where children learn a sense of ownership. (South Eastern Education and Library Board)

> I think the way the library is presented is all important, an attractive colour scheme, being welcomed at the door, inviting children and saying 'this is your library'. (Southwark)

This was highlighted by parents, too:

> Libraries are also seen as an appealing area for children, because they are a place in the community where you don't need money, a neutral space . . . libraries are one of the few places where children are actually made to feel welcome with bright child-friendly areas set aside.

> Displays of children's work are important in making them feel that the library is a place they have got a stake in.

The relative informality of the library environment, particularly in comparison to schools, is one of the strengths of the library service. Staff were seen as both approachable and knowledgeable – a potent mix when it comes to helping children in the selection of reading material:

> We get to know the children informally and that enables us to help them choose books that are right for them.

Often the innovative use of space and colour could overcome the effects of poor architectural design and old buildings. It was clear that libraries should be welcoming, appealing spaces. The environment was all important: this was not always a visual sensation, but could be the result of the more intangible effect of the ambience created by caring staff making the best of poor resources. Unfortunately it was still possible to find unattractive children's libraries, as noted by one teacher:

> . . . needs to be much more aesthetically pleasing and the layout should be better.

## Promotional management

Lack of money was seen as a prime inhibitor to the promotion of libraries and reading. It was recognized that library managers had become particularly adept at finding imaginative ways of circumventing budgeting problems. It was acknowledged that the funding base for promotional activities had diversified and expanded over recent years both internally and within the wider external context. Despite this diversification, the effects of budget cuts continued to be felt, and affected service provision in a number of ways:

- fewer staff, so less staff time to undertake promotion
- a lack of promotional budgets to support an adequate programme of events
- low training budgets which do not allow staff to acquire or improve skills
- the lack of external outreach work.

Library personnel in Scotland and Northern Ireland felt particularly cut off from UK national initiatives, and felt they had fewer opportunities to tap central sources of funding. The cutbacks had apparently had a more drastic effect in Wales than anywhere else, and authorities there were still reeling from the effects of local government reorganization three years previously. There was a need for a clearer framework to be developed so that library staff could make bids for funds to support specific local initiatives with adequate and appropriate support. Many staff were not aware of possible pots of funding even if they had sound and creative ideas which they could pursue.

One of the continuing features of promotional programmes was the establishment of partnerships between public libraries and other bodies to foster children's reading. These partnerships varied considerably, from a variety of localized business-based collaborations, to the take-up of large-scale projects on a national or even international scale. Key partners as indicated by the questionnaire survey continued to be other library authorities, teachers and schools, other local authority departments, and publishers. Much of the cooperation and partnership which had been undertaken in the past had tended to be ad hoc and unstructured.

Libraries were continually exploring avenues to discover new partners. Many of the libraries' traditional partners were experiencing contracting budgets – for example, in the booktrade – and were no longer able to provide as much support to libraries as previously. The diversification of the funding base for library-based initiatives has been a key feature in recent years, and the questionnaire survey supported this view of diversification. The range of funders, and the number of authorities accessing them for children's library service provision, was, however, still disappointingly low (see Table 5.4).

**Table 5.4**   *Percentage of authorities receiving external funding*

| | Counties | Met districts | London | Unitary author- ities | Wales | Scotland | NI | UK |
|---|---|---|---|---|---|---|---|---|
| European Union | 8.7 | 0 | 0 | 5 | 0 | 0 | 0 | 2 |
| Lottery | 4 | 4 | 0 | 5 | 0 | 0 | 0 | 2 |
| Local government | 13 | 36 | 12 | 21 | 5 | 4 | 0 | 15 |
| Other council depts | 17 | 24 | 35 | 42 | 24 | 15 | 0 | 25 |
| Local business | 61 | 40 | 31 | 37 | 19 | 42 | 25 | 38 |
| Local service organizations | 13 | 0 | 8 | 5 | 5 | 8 | 25 | 7 |
| Arts council | 30 | 4 | 15 | 26 | 52 | 81 | 75 | 36 |
| Regional arts boards | 57 | 32 | 8 | 26 | 10 | 0 | 0 | 21 |
| Other | 22 | 12 | 8 | 16 | 5 | 4 | 0 | 10 |
| No of respondents | 23 | 25 | 26 | 19 | 21 | 26 | 4 | 144 |

It was evident from Table 5.4 that the Arts Council and local business were key supporters of events in a considerable proportion of authorities. The support from local businesses for libraries was particularly heartening. It was disappointing that few authorities had yet sought European or lottery funding to support service developments in children's reading. Only 25% of authorities had received funding from other council departments, reinforcing the view that there was still a need to promote the library and its essential role in children's reading to other local authority departments – for example, education and social services.

## Evaluation and monitoring

The effective management of any programme of activities, as well as strategic planning, was clearly necessary to ensure the success of any initiatives. Evaluation and monitoring was clearly part of this:

> It is important to ensure that evaluation is built into the structure of the [marketing] plan's implementation; evaluation should be formative as well as summative and the plan should be flexible enough to accommodate change, if needed, at evaluation stages. Evaluation should not be treated as a snapshot for preservation, but as a tool for improving effectiveness. (De Saez, 1993, 133)

Libraries have increasingly had to use statistics as a management tool. Issue statistics, membership levels and the uptake of activities have all become more significant because they can be used to bargain for an increase in resourcing levels, but there is still a lack of anything other than the most superficial statistical gathering exercises. There was little evidence from case study authorities of any systematic evaluation of promotional events. The gathering of basic statistics was still the key evaluation method in use. This was supported by results from the questionnaire survey where, despite continued reference to the importance of this as a fundamental part of the marketing and promotional cycle in the literature, there were still a considerable number of authorities who did not undertake any detailed or systematic evaluation of events, despite the professional view which suggests:

> The importance of clear aims and objectives, plans for implementation, and clear evaluation are crucial to effectiveness in times of diminishing resources. (Blanshard, 1998, 15)

> While it is important to pre-plan with regard to promotion etc, it is important also to allocate time for monitoring and evaluation. This should not simply be an optional extra! (Eyre, 1994, 90)

The emphasis was placed squarely on matching achievements to the original objectives set. Metropolitan districts and authorities in Scotland were the most likely to undertake evaluation, and the low percentages for Northern Ireland, Wales and county authorities, as demonstrated in Table 5.5, were worrying.

Only isolated incidences of evaluation of specific promotional activities were identified through the questionnaire survey. These tended to centre on individual initiatives such as Brightstart, Bookstart and homework clubs. One might assume that a key component of the fight to justify service provision must be the in-depth gathering of meaningful statistics and qualitative evidence, but there was little evidence of the latter in either the questionnaire survey or the case study authorities. Authorities who choose to implement the Children's PLUS survey (CIPFA, 1998) may obtain some indication of children's perceptions of the quality of certain elements of service provision.

**Table 5.5**  *Percentage of authorities undertaking evaluation*

|  | % | Number of respondents |
|---|---|---|
| Counties | 18 | 22 |
| Metropolitan districts | 33 | 24 |
| London | 23 | 26 |
| Unitary authorities | 21 | 19 |
| Wales | 11 | 19 |
| Scotland | 35 | 20 |
| Northern Ireland | 0 | 3 |
| UK | 23 | 133 |

Justification of initiatives was a prime motivator for evaluation. Monitoring of events could lead to reassessment of priorities and objectives. Analysis of statistics led to one authority making a conscious decision to concentrate its efforts away from in-library storytimes and to use resources in the implementation of different initiatives:

> . . . storytimes do not reach that many children, they reach the same group and children time and again . . . we can use that resource in a much more productive way doing a range of different things.

It was possible for basic statistical evaluation to provide some lessons:

> Book Flood projects show that the more books you have, the greater the use.

Feedback mechanisms could be used to set up a useful dialogue with library users:

> For our summer promotion we got 319 comments forms back both from children and from parents.

Several authorities emphasized the need continually to reinforce and revisit promotion. There was an evident response from users in the wake of many promotional initiatives, but this interest was not sustained over time:

> . . . we realised the number of borrowers and loans increased after we had had a promotion and then fizzled off [sic] after a year.

## Specific promotional initiatives
## National initiatives

There have been a number of national initiatives in recent years in the area of children's reading. These include:

- Readathon, a sponsored reading event funded by the Roald Dahl Foundation
- National Children's Book Week, managed by Young Book Trust
- Reading is Fundamental, a series of projects which allow children to own books they choose themselves
- the government-funded National Year of Reading.

The inclusion of public libraries in the list of eligible organizations for arts-based National Lottery funding has also provided public libraries with increased opportunities for participation in events and the development of new programmes.

In a number of authorities there was a lack of awareness amongst staff of national initiatives which could potentially be linked to locally run projects. Amongst staff who were aware of their existence there was an underlying feeling that libraries could contribute considerably as part of these schemes. There was evidence that national initiatives could provide a forum or impetus for expansion and innovation in service development:

> The National Reading Initiative [sic] . . . is perhaps a better example of initiatives making a difference to our service, because I'm already putting together some ideas of what the library service would do in that year, and I'm negotiating with colleagues in the education department about how they could seek funding from their budgets to support that.

One of the key impacts of national initiatives was:

> . . . that we are reaching parents and carers much more systematically through nurseries, clinics and schools.

Particular concerns were expressed by library personnel regarding the sustainability of such events. There was an expressed need for monies provided by such sources to be used for pump priming rather than for the establishment of programmes which would not be sustainable beyond the limit of the initial funding. Notes of caution were expressed:

> We have to guard against bandwagon bidding. We need to bid for funding within a clear framework of what we want it for, why, how we are going to use it and how we will sustain it after the funding has ceased.

Not all staff agreed with the view that national initiatives had an impact on service development:

> *. . . virtually no impact from these initiatives.*

This was a disappointing view of a series of innovative initiatives with considerable potential for improving the library service for children and young people, particularly in the field of reading.

## Homework clubs

The questionnaire survey asked respondents to identify whether they offered any of a number of activities designed specifically to support children and their reading. Homework clubs were the most commonly offered (52%). This was possibly the result of a concern on the part of librarians that they were not adequately meeting the educational needs of children. Recent changes in educational policy, including the advent of more coursework-based assessment and the changed circumstances of school library services, have led to increased pressures on public library service provision. In some cases the development of homework support provided the opportunity to rationalize and focus resources to a particular area of need.

## Bookstart

The other initiative which authorities identified as important was Bookstart. Originally a cooperative initiative between Birmingham Library Services and Young Book Trust, Bookstart provided introductory book information packs (including a free book) to parents at their babies' eight-month development check. A significant feature of the project was the involvement of health visitors, who handed the packs to parents. This provided a model of cooperation between a number of agencies concerned with children's reading and development. The phenomenal uptake of Bookstart by other library authorities in the UK was a tribute to the high awareness of the project raised through effective promotion of the original project. The success of this initiative was discussed in research which documented the first five years of the original project (Wade and Moore, 1998). The significance of these projects rested in the way they reach children, via their parents, at a very young age. The potential for libraries to attract new borrowers, coupled with a firm commitment to the power of story, literacy and books in the life of the child, proved irresistible. The use of partners in the health service ensured the success of Bookstart, a scheme which could not operate with librarians alone.

## Family reading

Family reading groups also proved popular (20% of authorities). Their contribution to the promotion of reading was considerable. They could reach and influence both children and adults, and there were social benefits in providing an activity which whole families could undertake. There was also a possibility of breaking cycles of illiteracy by aiding children of parents with low-level literacy skills and motivating parents to improve their skills so they could support their children with their emerging skills, as noted by one teacher:

*Children's role in promoting adult reading is an issue in this community.*

## ICT

There was disappointingly little use of information and communications technology (ICT) as a means of promoting literacy in public libraries, although the advent of the Literacy Hour and the supporting Internet resources provided by the British Educational Communications and Technology Agency (BECTA) may change this. There were some innovative examples such as Stories on the Web, a joint project between the Birmingham, Leeds and Bristol library services and the UK Office for Library and Information Networking (UKOLN). This project links children to other children, both as readers and writers, and links children directly to authors.

There is considerable potential for ICT to be used as a tool for promoting and encouraging children's reading and as a tool for promoting the library in general. Library authorities were gradually providing a range of ICT facilities for children. These included CD-ROMs, Internet access, software loans and office software (Denham et al, 1996). Although there was some awareness of the possibility of the Internet as a means of promotion, this had not been explored in any depth in any of the case study authorities. A considerable amount of useful data was gathered and stored electronically by authorities. Leeds libraries had a detailed database of information on the 9000 children who had taken part in the Summer Reading Game in 1997. Birmingham libraries had used the database compiled as part of a survey of ethnic minority library users as the basis for a mailing list. There was considerable potential for the use of basic user information stored electronically, although few libraries had seen this potential and exploited it.

## Future plans and innovation

The questionnaire survey elicited responses about plans for future initiatives within individual authorities. Bookstart projects were mentioned by far more authorities than any other type of activity. This alone bears witness to what has been a very successful marketing project in its own right. The interest roused by Bookstart in a range of spheres has been considerable and has resulted in its take-up in a vast number of authorities. Other initiatives which appeared to be gaining pace around the country, and were being implemented by several authorities, were homework support clubs and IT-based initiatives.

Only a small number of authorities indicated that they were planning initiatives which might be considered as innovative. These included 'Roll on Reading – a literacy project to promote use of libraries by targeting children from ethnic minority communities, aged 3–8 years', designed to reach relatively young children and thus enabling a literacy habit to start early in life. Creative writing programmes, children's book festivals and reading groups featured in the future plans of some library authorities. Many of these activities have long been features of library service provision, but all are focused on the important area of literacy and the development of reading and writing skills.

The need to be constantly discovering and implementing new ideas to encourage reading was acknowledged by one respondent:

*You have to be looking for new ways to promote reading and new ways to hook into reluctant and keen readers.*

## Conclusions

Children's librarians continue to place the promotion of reading, books and literacy at the centre of service development, and this promotional activity was recognized as their forte. Innovative and well-organized activities programmes were implemented to support this core purpose, but there was a general need for a much more strategic approach to promotional work including full evaluation. Librarians were constantly searching for new perspectives on the promotion of reading and had considerable expertise and drive when pursuing these. Some of these new perspectives could be provided by a continued diversification of the funding base and a greater knowledge of the opportunities for project funding, particularly from lottery and European funding sources. There is need for librarians to develop new skills in the area of promotion, and one significant area which needs to be addressed is the potential of ICT to support reading and promotion. ICT could also be used as a vehicle for sharing good practice between authorities.

## References

Aslib (1995) *Review of public library services in England and Wales for the Department of National Heritage*, Aslib.

Blanshard, C (1997) *Children and young people: Library Association guidelines for public library services*, 2nd edn, Library Association Publishing.

Blanshard, C (1998) *Managing library services for children and young people: a practical handbook*, Library Association Publishing.

CIPFA (1998) *Children's PLUS: a national standard for surveying children and young people in public libraries and the community*, BLRIC/IPF.

Comedia (1993) *Borrowed time?: the future of public libraries in the UK*, Comedia.

De Saez, E (1993) *Marketing concepts for libraries and information services*, Library Association Publishing.

Denham, D (1997) Children and IT in public libraries: a research project, *Youth Library Review*, **23**, (Spring), 20–9.

Denham, D et al (1996) *Children and IT in public libraries*, British Library.

Eyre, G (1994) *Making quality happen: a practical guide to promoting your library*, Youth Libraries Group.

Eyre, G (1996), *Promoting libraries and literature for young people*. In Elkin, J and Lonsdale, R, *Focus on the child: libraries literacy and learning*, Library Association Publishing, 174–92.

Hill, J (1973) *Children are people: the librarian in the community*, Hamish Hamilton.

Kinnell, M (1996) *Meeting their needs: marketing and library services*. In Elkin, J and Lonsdale, R, *Focus on the child: libraries literacy and learning*, Library Association Publishing, 159–73.

Library and Information Services Council (England) Working Party on Library Services for Children and Young People (1995) *Investing in children: the future of library services for children and young people*, Library Information Series 22, HMSO.

Wade, B and Moore, M (1998) *Bookstart: five years on*, London, Book Trust.

CHAPTER 6

# Assessing services

## Peggy Heeks

Success is about our understanding what children and their
families need. (Chief Librarian)

## Introduction

The perception that public services should be accountable has grown steadily over the
past two decades. Indeed, the major reports on public librarianship noted in Chapter
1 – all published within the 1990s – call for even sharper attention to ways of measuring performance – that is, the performance of the library in delivering its various
services. The trend is clear, although emphasis, and the terminology which expresses
that emphasis, have changed. We have also become aware of the different perspectives
which need to be taken into account: those of the staff, the public and the politicians,
both national and local, who have particular funding responsibilities.

## Changing approaches to assessment
### Assessing effectiveness

This is a complex area – one where the various factors involved are closely intertwined,
and definitions are not always clear cut. The literature on the subject is extensive and
frequently so specialized that it is not easily accessible to practitioners. Basically, the
concern is with effectiveness, with ways of assessing that effectiveness and demon-
strating it, so an early definition may be helpful:

> The effectiveness of an organization is its ability to create acceptable outcomes and action
> . . . it reflects both an assessment of the usefulness of what is being done and of the

resources that are being consumed by the organization . . . (Pfeiffer and Salancik, 1978)

A later section of this chapter will consider the view of library effectiveness which emerged from the case studies. Effectiveness needs to be evaluated, and here a hierarchy of terms has become established, set out very clearly in *What's good: describing your public library's effectiveness* (Childers and Van House, 1993). The authors identify the following:

- *dimensions*, which are broad aspects of performance, for example 'administrative processes'
- *indicators*, which are specific items within a dimension, such as written policies
- *measures*, which are 'specific means of making indicators concrete'.

The major British manual on the subject is the weighty *Keys to success* (Griffiths and King, 1990), which builds on the American Library Association's *Performance measures for public libraries* (De Prospo, Altman and Beasley, 1973). The history of performance measurement in libraries shows a close association of interest between the UK and the USA. In both countries there has been a move from national to local standards, which take into account the needs and priorities of local communities – although in Britain there are hints of some pull-back from that position, in line with trends in education. There is a clear shift in focus from professional interests to user satisfaction, and consequently from a concentration on *inputs* (the resources allocated to the library) to measurement of *outputs* (service use) and consideration of *outcomes*, ie service impact and benefits.

Outputs and outcomes are much more difficult to assess. It is noticeable that manuals tend to peter out when it comes to suggesting outcome measures. Childers and Van House, for example, identified outputs and outcomes as posing exceptional problems:

> They are the least easily observed of all the elements of the system. They are often a product of not just the system under study but other, sometimes unknown, factors which may be far removed from the system in time and place. (Childers and Van House, 1993, 13)

## Quality management

The turning from a concentration on inputs to inclusion of a wider range of output and outcome measures signifies a growing interest in qualitative aspects, complementing the quantitative. This is manifest in the importance now accorded to quality management and quality assurance. The concept of quality management has received a boost through the establishment of the charter mark system, which is awarded to services of high quality, and from the work of Zeithaml, Parasuram and Berry (1990), who identified five aspects of service. These categories, known by the acronym RATER, cover:

- Reliability:          does the service meet set standards consistently?
- Assurance:          are staff knowledgeable, confident and courteous?
- Tangibles:          are the premises well designed, does equipment work?
- Empathy:          do users get attention that meets their needs?
- Responsiveness:    is the service prompt and helpful?

The major quality accreditation system available in the UK is BS 5750/ISO 9000, but this was designed originally for manufacturing industries and has not been taken up widely within the library and information services sector, where the Investors in People initiative, launched in 1994, appears to be more popular (Kinnell, 1997, 215–75). The quality management impetus has been seen mainly in library services to adults – which is to be expected, given its origins in the business world – but there is one manual developed specifically for work with children: *Output measures for public library service to children* (Walter, 1992).

As Walter admits, the measures described are predominantly quantitative. As part of the search for methods of service assessment, some librarians have turned to benchmarking, seeing it as a means of studying the leaders in specific aspects of service delivery and learning from them. In many ways, benchmarking can be seen as part of a natural progression from performance measurements and quality management systems.

## Planning

All these approaches to assessment have in common a belief in the value – indeed, necessity – of planning. School development plans have been advocated for nearly a decade (Hargreaves et al, 1989). A report on the public library service, *Due for renewal* (Audit Commission, 1997), highlights the need for 'rigorous service planning' and notes that some authorities lack any sort of planning process, while in other cases plans have internal weaknesses:

> Badly prepared plans can be counter-productive; well-prepared plans can position authorities to face the future with more confidence. (Audit Commission, 1997)

In the same year the Department of National Heritage also focused on planning in its response to the public library review, *Reading the future* (Department of National Heritage, 1997). From 1998 every library authority in England will be required to produce an annual plan, setting out its policies, services, targets and standards, plus a review of the previous year's achievement against targets. While the Department felt it inappropriate to set targets for authorities, it did list the performance indicators which should be used, and the Department of Culture, Media and Sport (DCMS) has now produced detailed guidelines for authorities.

Pressure for more transparent and rigorous methods of assessing services is growing, coming from both Government requirements and competition for funds. Public libraries will, therefore, be giving more attention to target setting and measurement, although we cannot expect one standard system to emerge. Information gathered in the course of A Place for Children confirms the following perception:

> In charting a path through the many definitions and components that comprise what is referred to as quality management, the diversity and contrast of approach is striking. (Milner, Kinnell and Usherwood, 1997, 131)

Whatever the approach, it will have been made easier by the advances in information and communications technology which make both collection of data and its manipulation much simpler.

## Service benefits

One of the starting points of A Place for Children was the following recommendation from the report *Investing in children*:

> Priority should be given to research which explores the benefits, impacts and effectiveness of library provision for children and young people. (LISC(E), 1995)

The core questions explored during the project included 'How do public libraries benefit children?' and all staff interviewed in the case studies were asked for their views on service benefits. It was also a topic for focus groups of teachers, parents and carers. This section draws particularly from these results.

## Access to materials

At the most obvious level, the library provides access to a wider range of books and related materials than is available in school or at home. The collection is available free, and was seen by parents as 'a cost-effective way of using public money'.

> *There's a tax for the library of about £11 a year, and for that we've got thousands of books, plus videos, tapes and CDs to borrow.*

The point was also made that the library's book collection is selected by specialists, according to policy guidelines, using criteria quite different from the best-seller priorities of commercial bookshops:

*This is one of the few places where children have equal and free access, without any pressure to buy.*

*We provide a safe and welcoming environment, where children come in their own right.*

## Reading development

The link between the library and reading development came through constantly:

*The public library is the driving force for children's reading development from the earliest age. The Bookstart projects have demonstrated this. The main justification for having a well-developed children's service is our role in encouraging reading.*

*We are enriching children's lives by fostering a love of reading, a love of learning and curiosity about life.*

Teachers spoke of library benefits in terms of extending children's reading interests and encouraging them to try new authors:

*Librarians spread enthusiasm, give you something you can take back to your class. The displays look so good, they immediately encourage you to take something new.*

*Coming to the library helps children's language and literacy development. Whether listening to a story or doing project work, they're practising and developing core reading skills.*

*The activities in the library benefit reading, spelling, general knowledge and creativity.*

Both the homework centres being established and the exercises included in class visits serve to improve information-handling skills, and there were good reports of family reading schemes:

*The family reading group has really benefited children's development. Children who would not normally speak up now seem quite happy to talk about the books they like to read in front of a group of people.*

Research has shown that children's attitudes to books and reading are strong indicators of their eventual school progress; and this aspect of library benefits was another recurring theme:

*The public library reinforces what takes place in schools, by developing favourable attitudes to books, creating a reading environment.*

*We model adult and child sharing of the enjoyment of books. That's important to parents as well as the children.*

## Corporate policy development

Chief librarians spoke of political understanding of the benefits of service to children, which in some cases linked with corporate policies such as the aim of 'developing people for life' or promoting equal opportunities. There has also been national recognition:

> Libraries provide an important opportunity for young people to develop reading and a love of books, the first rung of the ladder to literacy and learning throughout life. (Department of National Heritage, 1997)

As the Education Secretary launched targets for the National Year of Reading in 1998, he spoke of the contribution public libraries had to offer in bringing about 'a sea of change in the nation's attitude to reading'.

## Spreading the word

The important benefits of children's library services have been perceived by all the authorities case studied for A Place for Children – with both Leeds and Northamptonshire achieving substantial budget increases for this work – but news of those benefits needs to be shared more widely. It is significant that a specialist whose service was showing increases of 30% picked up this point:

> *We're making a really major contribution to literacy development yet somehow there's a lack of confidence that what we're doing is worth sharing.*

## Service effectiveness

Effectiveness has been defined as 'impact on the consumer or user' (Childers and Van House, 1993, 5). It is, therefore, particularly concerned with outputs and outcomes, service aspects which were explored during the case studies through specific questions on assessment of the impact of children's services and on methods of assessing success. A high proportion of the answers focused on customer satisfaction. Evidence of this was seen partly in the issue figures. It is significant that loans of children's books have increased overall in the past few years, while those of adult fiction have declined. Behind that record lies intensive professional effort, and it is, perhaps, time that we reassessed the importance of issue figures. They are a clear indicator of satisfaction, for they represent continuing use from readers who return week after week. Participation in summer book trails was also seen as an indicator of effectiveness, and the trend here, too, was upward, with Leeds outstanding in tripling the number of children taking part in its 1997 Reading Game.

Impact was perceived in children's comments on the books they read or the stories they were told. These experiences were ongoing and hard to quantify, but their influence was seen in children's writing and art work displayed in the library. Librarians talked of the importance of 'customer closeness', of building good relationships:

> *The demand by children shows success. Sometimes children come in to say thank you, or to tell you their project got a merit at school, and then you know you've done a good job. You can see word of mouth working in the street.*

> *You know you're having an impact when a child comes in asking 'Can we have that book you talked about at school, Miss?'.*

> *I believe that we do have evidence of success. Partly it comes from awareness of how children feel about the library. As I walk through a child will say 'Hello, you came to my school. I've got this book now.' They really feel it's their library and a good place to be. Children want to come to events and join in. It's their faces as they go that provide the evidence. 'Goodbye, we've had a lovely time'.*

The case study libraries did, however, use more formal ways of getting children's views through user surveys and comments forms. The remark of one chief librarian might serve for all:

> *Success is about our understanding what children and their families need.*

The library service in Leeds was helped by a city-wide survey by the city council of the views of children and young people, *Leeds listens* (Leeds City Council, 1996), but it is increasingly common for library departments to carry out user surveys. There are obvious problems in gathering children's views, and the work on producing a standard methodology has been welcomed (Gordon and Griffiths, 1997, 372–4). The bulk of comments on children's services are gathered from parents and teachers – for example, through evaluation of summer reading programmes, book fairs and class visits.

Hampshire cited testimonials from parents on its Family Library Link, and the independent evaluation of the Early Years project:

> *We see differences in the children over a 2–3-year period of use; in attention span, in knowledge of authors, in selection skills.* (Hampshire)

Leeds carried out a survey among schools about the effectiveness of its 1997 summer reading promotion, and 63% of teachers felt that their children had progressed more in their reading than they would have expected.

In two authorities the demand from schools for class visits outstripped capacity. Another had started a summer mobile service to rural areas, with storytelling at each stop, and had received a host of requests from parents and teachers for its repetition. In another area, a local primary school was paying staff costs of an additional weekly visit.

> *When the new library was established some distance away, few children used it. They had previously made regular visits to the library in our grounds. Reading levels dropped and we felt we had to respond. So we started a programme of regular visits. Reading levels of the past three years show the impact. We now have more children reading at higher levels, and fewer in special needs groups. The improvement in reading skills has had a good effect on other subjects too. The increases are small but steady. We have to educate the parents too, about the importance of the library. That is working slowly and shows in the increase in children visiting the library during the holidays on their own account. The school visits establish the habit. Our children are rarely given books as presents. The library gives them a favourable attitude to books that will be life-long. It extends their range. P6/7 children have just been reading A secret garden which was quite a challenge. The same year group is also using the library for project work, for example, on the Victorians.*

Some chief librarians pointed out that the effectiveness of the service was reflected in staff morale and confidence, but this was set in a more objective context by continuing assessment of their service. Croydon, for example, has an annual consideration of its Book Trail programme:

> *It's easy to drift on, making assumptions. We always consider the justification for any activity.*
> (Croydon)

Core library operations are monitored regularly in several places, with weekly meetings of library managers, quarterly reports, or service audits by senior staff, all designed to assess effectiveness. Such systems serve as a reminder that library activity should be set within a planning process:

> *You have to be clear about what you are setting out to do. It is definition at the front that helps you define the success factors, the way to measure at the end.*

## Policy statements

In the case studies there were outstanding examples of the integration of purpose and outcome, linked with systematic monitoring. However, the overall picture gives cause for concern. The questionnaire responses show only 30% of authorities with a policy statement for services to children and young people, and only 26% with promotional policies for them. This is in line with findings reported in *Due for renewal* (Audit Commission, 1997, 50) that planning requires more attention.

Given current budget restrictions and reductions in the number of specialists, it is equally perturbing that questionnaire responses show an imbalance between what libraries do and what they regard as very important in terms of promotion of reading. For example, 70% provide magazines for children, but only 25% think them very important; 63% provide posters, but only 8% rate them highly; nearly half provide toys and games, but only 5% think them important. There is a case for much closer scrutiny of activities to decide which are effective, and there were signs in the interviews that this was beginning. Were class visits being used to best advantage? Should they be more closely linked to current project work and reading development? Only 39% of respondents thought it very important to support the formal education provided by schools, yet over 50% supported homework, and 75% thought promoting literacy was of the highest importance:

*We have activities and programmes rather than a strategy.*

## Performance indicators and measures

There is now considerable literature on performance indicators and measures, and it may be helpful to step back from the often complex detail to look at their purpose. 'Performance indicators help [professionals] to establish priorities' (Carbone, 1995). The library manager seeks to balance quality and economy, to provide a service of high quality in a way that uses services efficiently. Currently there is a search for indicators that can help assessment of service at both quantitative and qualitative levels, but there is also a recognition that our existing tools offer only limited views of library effectiveness (Childers and Van House, 1993, 16). Kinnell notes that performance measurement to monitor library effectiveness 'has often been of the most rudimentary quantitative type' (Kinnell, 1997). This point is borne out by the performance indicators the Audit Commission requires library authorities to collect.

In *Due for renewal*, library authorities were required by the Audit Commission (1997) to collect the following performance indicators in 1996–7:

- issues per capita of books and of other items
- the number of books and recordings available in libraries per capita
- number of public libraries open 45 hours or more per week and open 10–44 hours per week, and the number of mobile libraries
- number of visits per capita
- expenditure per capita on books and other materials
- net expenditure per capita.

*Reading the future* (Department for National Heritage, 1997, Annex) added to this list several additional indicators which should be used from 1998:

1 **Efficiency:**
   - issues per lending item in stock (by category – adult fiction and non-fiction, children, audio, video)
   - net expenditure per loan
   - total expenditure and income per capita
   - % of total expenditure on materials (by category – adult fiction and non-fiction, children, audio, video) and staff costs.

2 **Access and usage:**
   - book issues per capita
   - other media issues (by category – audio (music), audio (talking book), CD-ROMs and computer software, online and electronic media) per capita
   - % of requests supplied within seven days and within 30 days
   - reference enquiries per capita
   - % of opening hours outside 'office hours' (say, 9am–5pm)
   - % of total population who are library members
   - % of under-14-year-olds who are library members
   - % of library members who are active borrowers (ie who have borrowed in the preceding 12 months)
   - % of (eligible) people requesting housebound services who receive them..

The Chartered Institute of Public Finance and Accountancy (CIPFA) also collects public library statistics, and a survey carried out at CIPFA's request showed 'a widespread demand for more defined statistics'. The resulting proposals (Sumsion and Creaser, 1996, 22) show considerable similarity to the Department of National Heritage recommendations.

## Additional indicators

Taking these nationally recognized indicators as a whole, it is clear that they do not provide a sufficient guide to the effectiveness of services to children. Some of the project respondents were already collecting statistics in addition to the Audit Commission requirements which reflected significant aspects of service to children, such as attendance at library events. Just occasionally – for example, in Bexley and Knowsley – the indicators were linked with specific targets. Redbridge collected details of children finishing club activities as well as joining them. This emerged as important information in assessing performance given the prevalence of summer reading clubs and book trails. It is a reminder that it is not enough to launch an activity: its progress needs to be monitored, the results evaluated, and amendments made as necessary.

The most detailed guide to the assessment of children's library services comes in *Output measures for public library service to children* (Walter, 1992, 2) and its summary is reproduced below. Walter's proposals were field-tested as part of the Public Library Development Program in the USA.

## Overview of the measures
### Library use

1   *Children's library visits per child* is the average number of visits to the library by people age 14 and younger per child (14 and younger) in the community served. It measures walk-in use of the library.
2   *Building use by children* indicates the average number of people 14 and under who are in the library at any particular time. Together with *Children's library visits per child*, this measure shows patterns of use.
3   *Furniture/equipment use by children* measures the proportion of time, on average, that a particular type of furniture or equipment, such as pre-school seating or computer terminals, is in use by people 14 and under.

### Materials use

These measures reflect the extent to which the library's collection is used:

1   *Circulation of children's materials per child* measures the use of children's library materials loaned for use outside the library, relative to the number of people age 14 and under in the service area.
2   *In-library use of children's material per child* indicates the use of children's library materials within the library, relative to the number of people age 14 and under in the community served.
3   *Turnover rate of children's materials* indicates the intensity of use of the children's collection, relating the circulation of children's materials to the total size of the children's collection.

### Materials availability

These measures, all variants of *fill rates*, reflect the degree to which children and their care givers are able to find materials they want during their visits to the library:

1   *Children's fill rate* is the percentage of searches for library materials by users age 14 and under, and adults acting on behalf of children, that are successful.

2   *Homework fill rate* is the proportion of searches for information and/or library materials for homework use by library users age 14 and under, and adults acting on behalf of children, that are successful.

3   *Picture book fill rate* is the percentage of searches for picture books that are successful.

## Information services

Information services help the client use information resources and provide answers to specific questions. Information services include both reference and readers' advisory services:

1   *Children's information transactions per child* is the number of information transactions by library users age 14 and under, and adults acting on behalf of children, per person age 14 and under in the community served.

2   *Children's information transaction completion rate* is the percentage of information transactions by persons age 14 and under, and by adults acting on behalf of children, that are completed successfully.

## Programming

Library staff provide programmes that inform, educate, motivate, and entertain children and their care givers as well as promote library use:

1   *Children's program attendance per child* measures annual attendance at children's library programmes per person age 14 and under in the community served.

## Community relations

Children's services staff work actively with schools, child care centres, and other community organizations and agencies that serve children and youth. These measures quantify much of the work that is done in the community:

1   *Class visit rate* measures visits from school classes to the library relative to the total number of school classes in the community.

2   *Child care centre contact rate* is the number of contacts between the library and child care centres relative to the number of child care centres in the community.

3   *Annual number of community contacts* is the total number of community contacts made by library staff responsible for service to children during the year.

## Developing indicators

If we are to make progress in developing similar measures in the UK, collaboration in designing the measures is needed – bringing in agencies such as the Library Association, CIPFA and the Library and Information Statistics Unit with a task group of practitioners under the aegis of a research institution – plus provision for field-testing them. Such leadership is needed if performance assessment of children's services is to be more effective and more widespread. Research carried out in 1994–5 found that 86% of public library departments responding were using performance indicators (Garrod and Kinnell, 1997) – a very different result from that obtained from A Place for Children respondents, where only 36% answered affirmatively to the question 'Do your libraries use performance indicators to evaluate your work in the area of children's and teenagers' reading?'

As part of the case study interviews, heads of library service were asked 'What importance do you attach to performance measurement in your service?' and 'What measures do you use to assess success in promotion of children's reading?' Similar questions were put to heads of children's services. Three particular points emerged. The first was that performance indicators were seen as valuable management tools – or, at least, potentially valuable. The information collected needed interpreting and integrating in service planning. The second was that authorities were already using a range of measures:

*Secondary measures are helpful: good behaviour, a lack of vandalism, a lack of complaints.*

*We pay great attention to client comments. We had over 300 comments from our summer programme; we get teachers' evaluation of class visits.*

*Monitoring of performance is built into our client-customer specifications.*

The use of focus groups, and surveys of users and non-users on the lines of the CIPFA-PLUS methodology, was growing, albeit slowly. The third main finding was that heads of service overall felt that attention to performance would increase:

*We are just at the starting block of performance measurement. We are using new membership figures: 3,000 of the 9,000 children taking part in the summer reading programme were new members. We look at press coverage in terms of column inches . . . And you also need to look at the qualitative, the quotes from people who care about children, and the quotes from the children themselves. With the facts and figures you get a rich mosaic of assessment.*

There were also several reminders that the statistics are telling us something important about service impact. In many cases they are very impressive:.

*We shouldn't knock the quantitative. In some cases it's the most appropriate measure.*

Service performance can be measured in several ways: over time, against targets set, in comparison with other authorities, and against average figures. All these methods received support in the case studies. There was a call for in-depth longitudinal studies. There was emphasis on the need to set activities within a clear framework of service objectives, and also to have high expectations of what can be achieved. There were tributes to the value of the LISU surveys of children's services in showing service levels elsewhere.

## Benchmarking

There was acknowledgment of the value, in principle, of benchmarking. Benchmarking has been defined as:

> The continuous process of measuring products, services and practices against lenders, allowing the identification of best practices which will lead to superior practice. (Garrod and Kinnell, 1997)

The problem for some library managers was finding comparable authorities. For example, Hampshire did not find benchmarking useful:

> *No other authority is really similar. Essex has 100 service points; we have 54. Our territory is completely different from Kent or Lancashire, and so are our reader expectations.* (Hampshire)

Croydon, on the other hand, saw benchmarking as something more than a means of comparison:

> *It can be used as a means of asking questions, or giving a different way of looking at service standards. We do get something from keeping in touch with authorities in the same family group.* (Croydon)

Croydon was part of the South East London Performance Indicators Group, some of whose members were addressing children's services specifically. It is through groups such as these, the Library Association, and the Public Libraries Research Group, that a forum could be created to look at valid practitioner-based performance indicators. Certainly interest was expressed during the case studies in some action research on these lines. The Library Association guidelines for service to children and young people (Blanshard, 1997) and the proposals of *Reading the future* (Department of National Heritage, 1997, Annex) offer a starting point. The studies for A Place for Children provide a context.

## Social factors

There is a growing recognition of the importance of social factors in assessing the performance of both schools and libraries. Judgments need to take into account the areas they serve. The case studies showed up some of the diversity. There were towns where the library attracted a high children's membership, helped by parents who turned naturally to books. There were areas of deprivation where reading and book borrowing were not part of the culture:

*We have to work really hard to get issues. Even so, we come out below average.*

Results below national average may still represent great achievement for a library. Assessment without regard to the social setting becomes simplistic. Gradually, the library profession is drawing attention to the social role of libraries. *New library: the people's network* sees public libraries 'at the hub of the community', 'nurturing social cohesion'. Among the five roles identified is one related to community history and identity (Library and Information Commission, 1997, ii, 2). A review of theoretical issues in the social impact of UK public libraries makes the case for including social impact when considering effectiveness, and urges a need for more sensitive tools for measuring it:

Quantitative assessments do not tell us all we need to know about the social function public libraries perform. (Kerslake and Kinnell, 1997, 8)

As a contribution to National Libraries Week 1997, the Library Association brought together substantial information on the social role of libraries. Apart from the literature review cited above, a national survey was carried out, which found that over half of responding authorities were involved in community development at a strategic level, and that activities included several relating to children – for example, study centres, literacy programmes, Share a Book initiatives (McKrell, Green and Harris, 1998). Comedia reviewed library-based schemes submitted for the Library Association/Holt Jackson Community Initiative Award 1992–97, which included a number focused on children (Matarosso, 1998). In addition, Bob Usherwood and Rebecca Linley developed tools for conducting a social audit of public library service (Usherwood and Linley, 1998). Their respondents identified the value of the public library as a resource for children, as a place where people meet, interact and share common interests.

A Place for Children has produced evidence of the wide range of library activities which make for community well-being: over 26% of respondents support Bookstart projects, 50% offer homework support, 20% provide intensive support through a Bookbus initiative, and a similar percentage support family reading groups. The social influence of the public library is, however, even more pervasive. The library was often a symbol of security in areas of little hope:

> *The library is a haven of resources, especially as a social space in a desolate area. Roaming stray dogs, broken windows, peeling paint, characterise the landscape. The library truly belongs to this community and children are being socialised as well as offered reading materials.*

Teachers commented that class visits were part of children's social development.

> *They help children feel part of the community and at ease in a major community resource. This is reinforced by the strong links the library makes with parents.*

Librarians and teachers spoke of the social development which comes from familiarity with a public environment:

> *There's the important experience of being part of a group sharing stories, and learning to move around the building with confidence.*

A mother commented of her toddler:

> *He knows his way around. He likes it here, feels comfortable.*

At the other end of the age range, some library departments were concentrating on the information needs of teenagers, where the library offered 'a neutral ground', free from fears of being overlooked. Library use helped the development of responsible attitudes and social awareness, bringing experience of a whole range of relationships: collective experience on a class visit or at a storytelling session; experience of engaging with adults who were neither parents nor teachers; the individual experience of engaging with literature. The observation undertaken as part of the project confirmed children's enjoyment of the library and its programmes, and the efforts of staff to make them feel welcome:

> *This is a warm, safe place, where children learn a sense of ownership. They come in after school, read stories to one another, listen to tapes. Children look to the library as a kind of social centre.*

The independent evaluation of Hampshire's Early Years initiative found the library environment even more important than the services offered, and this care to create the right atmosphere was apparent throughout the case studies, confirming the comment of one children's librarian:

> *The children really feel it's their library and a good place to be.* (Hampshire)

## Conclusions

The limitations of our current methods of assessing children's services are implicit in some of the developments noted above. A Place for Children has confirmed the present inadequacy and this chapter has offered suggestions for ways of addressing the task of designing qualitative indicators.

The complexity of the subject is a continuing theme in the subject literature. We read of 'the multi-dimensionality of effectiveness and validity of multiple viewpoints', and the need to use 'both a paint-by-number and impressionism' to produce a whole picture of library effectiveness (Childers and Van House, 1993, 7, 12). It is pointed out that 'even if measurement were possible, it would be difficult to isolate the library service's contribution' (Lancaster, 1993). As in so many disciplines, definition of terms lacks consistency. A salutary article 'Measuring the impact of information' looks at the relationship between data, information and knowledge, and the multiple meanings of 'impact'.

> Impact can only be measured or detected by the most subtle or restrictive and probably unreliable of tests. (Meadows and Weijing, 1997)

The case studies show practitioners much in accord with academics over this issue:

> We need to paint more real life pictures as in New library's stories of Susan and Zahir.

> We don't look at the individual side enough. We need to work through case-studies of individuals.

There was a concern that the profession had been 'too obsessed with statistics', and that gathering more might be counterproductive:

> We are constantly evaluating our services, but so much of what libraries do cannot be expressed in numbers. All the statistics won't show how you've changed children's lives. With the homework clubs we are measuring the impact by asking parents, schools and the children themselves, but this can be counter-productive. Homework clubs are meant to be different from schools. If you then try to measure in terms of improvement of academic performance, it becomes just another area where children are assessed.

> How do you measure the effect of someone reading a book? The impact may be far-reaching in emotional, social or intellectual terms. We have to take impact largely on trust. We are offering children and parents a quality experience which must have some impact.

Regular assessment of library services to children can be a means of raising standards. It is also part of the process of public accountability and of maintaining or increasing support for the work. This chapter has shown the trend towards using a range of approaches to service assessment. As library managers identify the key stakeholders, they need to decide which approach will speak most effectively to each.

## References

Audit Commission (1997) *Due for renewal: a report on the library service*, Audit Commission.

Blanshard, C (1997) *Children and young people: Library Association guidelines for public library services*, 2nd edn, Library Association Publishing.

Carbone, P (1995) The committee draft of International Standard ISO CD 11620 on Library Performance Indicators, *IFLA Journal*, **21**, 274–6.

Childers, T and Van House, N A (1993) *What's good: describing your public library's effectiveness*, American Library Association.

De Prospo, E R, Altman, E and Beasley, K E (1973) *Performance measures for public libraries*, American Library Association.

Department of National Heritage (1997) *Reading the future: a review of public libraries in England*, HMSO.

Garrod, P and Kinnell, M (1997) Towards library excellence: best practice benchmarking in the library and information sector. In Brockman, J (ed), *Quality management and benchmarking in the information sector: results of recent research*, Bowker Saur, 307–98.

Gordon, J and Griffiths, V (1997) *A national poll for children*, Library Association Record, 99 (7).

Griffiths, J M and King, D W (1990) *Keys to success: performance indicators for public libraries*, Office of Arts and Libraries.

Hargreaves, D et al (1989) *Planning for school development: advice to governors, headteachers and teachers*, Department of Education and Science.

Kerslake, E. and Kinnell, M (1997) *Public libraries, public interest and the information society*, BLRIC report 85, Library Association, Community Service Group.

Kinnell, M (1997) Quality management. In Mackenzie, G and Feather, J, *Librarianship and information work worldwide, 1996/97*, Bowker-Saur, 251–75.

Lancaster, F W (1993) *If you want to evaluate your library*, 2nd edn, Library Association Publishing.

Library and Information Commission (1997) *New library: the people's network*, Library and Information Commission.

Library and Information Services Council (England) Working Party on Library Services for Children and Young People (1995), *Investing in children*, HMSO.

Matarosso, F (1998) *Beyond book issues: the social potential of library projects*, BLRIC report 87, Comedia.

McKrell, L, Green, A and Harris, K (1998) *Libraries and community development*, BLRIC

Report 86, Library Association, Community Development Foundation and Community Services Group.

Meadows, C and Weijing, Y (1997) Measuring the impact of information studies, *Information Processing and Management,* **33** (6), 699–714.

Milner, E, Kinnell, M and Usherwood, R (1997) Quality management and public library services: the right approach? In Brockman, J (ed), *Quality management and benchmarking in the information sector: results of recent research,* Bowker Saur.

Pfeiffer, J and Salancik, G R (1978) *The external control of organizations,* Harper & Row.

Sumsion, J and Creaser, C (1996), *LISU review of CIPFA public library statistics,* Loughborough University Library and Information Statistics Unit.

Usherwood, B and Linley, R (1998) *New measures for the new library: a social audit of public libraries,* BLRIC report 89, University of Sheffield Centre for the Public Library in the Information Society.

Walter, V A (1992) *Output measures for public library service to children: a manual of standardized procedures,* American Library Association.

Zeithaml, V A, Parasuram, A and Berry, L L (1990) *Delivering quality service: balancing customer perceptions and expectations,* Free Press.

# CHAPTER 7

# Overview and summary of findings

Judith Elkin

## Introduction

More than anything else, the research reflected in this book showed overwhelmingly how public libraries can support children's development, improving their reading skills and helping them to grow intellectually, socially and culturally. Many parents, children, librarians and teachers believed this. But it was a message that had not been trumpeted. The policy makers and politicians at local and national government levels had failed to grasp the hugely significant role of libraries in the future shaping of the nation's children. This book has attempted to show some of the excellent work going on, but the vision for the future needs grasping now by politicians, educators and the library profession.

Children are complex individuals growing up in a rapidly changing world. Books and literacy are important for early development and lifelong learning, even in today's technological age. Early access to stories and to books is an essential part of the child's pre-reading experience and needs reinforcing as they become sophisticated readers, learners and thinkers. The role of libraries is paramount in supporting the child's reading and ensuring equitable access to all, regardless of age, gender, race, wealth, physical or intellectual ability, or geographical location. In addition to working with books, librarians are responding to the challenges brought about by the 'information age'. Media and technology impact hugely on the development of the child and have had a significant impact on publishing for children. Provision of multimedia, audiovisual and computer technology, in addition to the printed word, are the prerequisites for developing library services to children of the 21st century. Children's libraries now and in the future must have a remit to respond to established media and the emergence of new technologies both through their collections and their services.

The public library provides the only statutory local government service available to children from babyhood to adolescence. Yet there has never been an assessment of its value. A Place for Children attempted to remedy this by undertaking a major investigation into the qualitative impact of public libraries on children's reading and development. It is the most far-reaching piece of research into library services to children ever mounted in the United Kingdom. It was ambitious in its scope, covering England, Northern Ireland, Scotland and Wales, and in its focus, the impact of public libraries on children's reading and development.

The research began with the view that library services for children and young people were a key national asset in supporting children's reading needs, a tremendous resource unlike any other. In focusing the study on public libraries' roles in supporting children's reading, we emphasized that reading development was key to children's success. The special, indeed unique, place of the public library in reading development gave us the title for the study and summarized our intention of trying to demonstrate a continuing role for children's public libraries into the next millennium. The case studies provided some inspirational examples, with particular evidence of social impact and a safe haven.

During the research, parents and teachers were asked for their responses to the public library, and indicated overwhelmingly that libraries are key supporters of children's reading and are particularly good at emphasizing the idea that reading is fun, rather than a chore to be learned at school. Public libraries are clearly places for children, with materials and professional expertise that uniquely enable children and young people to unlock the door to their reading and hence to their social, intellectual and emotional development. Particular groups which are currently being targeted by libraries are the under-fives, teenagers and children with special needs.

The research was carried out during a period of some turbulence for public services. A Place for Children showed the very direct effects of such turbulence on the managers and front-line staff, who strive to maintain, and even improve, services. It was a time of changeover from a long-standing Conservative government to a new Labour government. The Labour Party's election rallying cry in 1997 was 'Education, Education, Education'. Since then, there has been evidence that education at all levels has been a priority for the government. Initiatives such as literacy hours in schools, lifelong learning, the National Year of Reading, homework clubs, and the potential of ICT through the National Grid for Learning and the public library network, now pervade national, regional and local thinking. Particular focuses of government concern are social inclusion, access, economic value and open government. All such initiatives potentially have a significant impact on libraries, literacy and learning.

## The child

The research for A Place for Children reinforced our view of the child as individual and the need to recognize the diversity of children, with their very different reading needs at differing stages of development and in different home and geographical environments. The library caters for all, providing inclusion and access to children regardless of age, wealth, background, gender, race, environment or geographical location. It supports lifelong reading and learning, offers individuals the opportunity to become members for life, and gives children equal status as well as providing them with a social space of their own.

Particular groups highlighted in the research as being a current focus for libraries were:

## Under-fives

For under-fives, the public library is the only statutory service, and is available to all children and their parents or carers. It is unique where pre-school children are concerned. It can be the most significant stimulus to reading that pre-school children experience, providing books and information from birth.

## Under-sevens

In learning to read, children are assimilating everything they need for life. This can make a significant difference to their future development. Exposure to books and libraries during their early years is critical, to ensure support in terms of their wider reading as children develop emerging reading skills.

## Special needs

Libraries are also a facility where mainstream children go. Special needs children can mix with other children and learn how to behave in the library environment, so that they are introduced to an important community facility. Libraries may offer special collections, eg for dyslexia or giant picture books (for the visually impaired).

## Boys

More boys than girls experience reading failure. This can tip over later into the adult education service, where young men present themselves for basic skills sessions, or maybe never recover from this. Libraries, through knowledge of the right books at the right time or promoting reading through IT, can support and nurture poor or reluctant readers.

## Home-educated children

One of the areas where libraries have been making significant impact is the whole area of home education. For many families and children, the mainstream education system does not work or is not what they are looking for. The library service can have a direct benefit because it can provide materials, resources, facilities, activities and services specifically targeted at home education. Children educated at home have the chance in the library to meet their peers and to fit into the world in a more structured way. For many home-educated children, parents value quiet study space in a bookish, focused atmosphere away from television.

## Ethnic minority children

Many children in the black community are still failing. In some libraries, they are seen as a priority, not because they are black but because like some white children the education system is failing them. One library spelt out their pleasure that, although the local adult Bangladeshi community did not use the library much, their children were beginning to. The library provided an important route to language and social integration for ethnic minority communities. Again, the library, through careful stock selection, can ensure that black and Asian children are shown as being valued and welcomed.

## Teenagers

Teenagers have very specific information needs and the library offers a neutral ground where they can find information without being overlooked or commented on. They hear a lot about drugs, about sex, about gender, but are often poorly informed about the facts and rights and wrongs. In a subtle way, by making leaflets available, the library provides a valuable service.

## Role of libraries

Every child needs the library: children are the future movers and shakers of the nation. Reading has a value in children's personal, social and imaginative development. The library provides children with a rare opportunity to choose for themselves and an opportunity for self-expression and discrimination. Children are able to grow up with books around them. Getting children into the library used to be seen as a problem, but many libraries now report that, once children have been introduced to the library, and they see for themselves what is on offer, they stay. Clearly the fact that children keep coming back is important; the library is, after all, a place where children go voluntarily. The library was seen as doing enriching work: enriching lives by fostering a love of reading; encouraging children to be curious about life. Welcoming, attractive libraries, with vibrant stock, were seen as important to children's reading. Children need to feel valued and *they won't if you give them old bookstock and just assume you know what is best*. One authority, where a refurbishment programme had been carried out, noted a 32% increase in issue figures. There is also a social benefit from the relationship with library staff. In Edinburgh, libraries are seen to be a vital part of Scottish culture.

## Quality of life

The library service benefits the quality of life. One library authority stated that:

> *Assessing the benefits of public libraries is an old problem. You know libraries are a good thing, and people will tell you that they are, but you can't measure their effects. We have to accept that in a civilised society certain things are valuable...we have an expectation of excellence, and of telling people that we are. The culture breeds a confidence. Over the last ten years, children's [book] issues have gone up, holding against alternative forms of education and entertainment which have taken off in that time.* (Hampshire)

## Citizenship

Libraries offer children a first right of citizenship:

> *We offer them the library membership card which belongs to them, the first thing they own for themselves. We also meet children before they get to school, so in terms of early learning and early education, libraries have a direct benefit.*

> *Library membership creates a sense of belonging and citizenship at an early age.*

> *Libraries are often the first formal organisation children come into contact with. They are the first places where children are treated as independent, so it gives them the chance to learn the rules of behaviour, to learn the correct behaviour in different situations.*

## Social development

Croydon libraries emphasized the social role of libraries:

> *We enable children to set time aside for sharing something enjoyable in an intimate, caring environment. We model adult–child sharing, and make parents and carers aware of the value of books. Visits to the library and sharing books are part of the social development of the child.* (Croydon)

Particularly for those children where things might not be going well elsewhere, libraries can have a long-term sustainable impact on a child's quality of life into adulthood. In some deprived areas with a lot of social problems and single parents, the library becomes a haven:

> . . . a social space in a pretty desolate area: roaming stray dogs, broken windows, peeling paint characterise the landscape . . . library as social space and the security to meet their friends on neutral, well-regulated territory.

This was a case study in an area where the library truly belonged to the community and children were being socialized as well as offered reading materials and information. Their observed behaviour in the library was generally reasonable, but the children demanded considerable attention and tended to lapse into attention-seeking behaviour, leading the researcher observing them to ask: 'But how often do such children have the individual attention of an adult in other settings?' In contrast in the library, children were talked to, asked about themselves, given crayons to colour in pictures and shown how to use the computers.

## Socially inclusive

The library was perceived as having a role as an agent to counteract social exclusion:

> Reading develops social awareness and the library provides children with a rare opportunity to choose for themselves and opportunities for self-expression and discrimination.

A number of authorities, such as Southwark, have very distinctive and often contrasting communities which do not necessarily mix very well:

> That's where the libraries can benefit children in fostering their socialisation skills and by giving them access to communities other than their own . . . We are certainly rigorous in applying our equal opportunities policy and we won't tolerate any discrimination within our libraries.

## A welcoming environment

The provision of a welcoming and non-threatening environment was seen as being of prime value:

> We're providing a context, which is non-threatening, non-judgmental.

Libraries are seen as a place in the community where you don't need money – a neutral space. Libraries are one of the few places where children are actually made to feel welcome with bright child-friendly areas set aside:

*This is a warm safe place where children learn a sense of ownership. They come in after school, read stories to one another, listen to tapes. Children look to the library as a kind of social centre.*

*We try to make it comfortable for them, away from the restrictions like 'don't touch, don't speak'*

As the mother of one toddler said:

*He knows his way around. He likes it here, feels comfortable.*

In small communities, the library is often the centre of the community, a community resource for children. The emphasis was on encouraging ownership of their library. At one library in Edinburgh, a reading garden was created outside, to encourage a sense of ownership – this resulted in the environment locally being changed.

The poignancy expressed by one librarian working on an estate in Northern Ireland, in the highest area of unemployment in the UK, spells out the issues involved:

*You have only to look around to see the need of a library. This estate has been ravaged by the troubles, there is no home environment of books, there is low educational aspiration. There is no bookshop and no book buying tradition. The library works closely with schools in promoting literacy. Here they have access to a free source of information and inspiration. We build on the strong oral tradition that still exists. The children have good listening skills and we connect with these roots by myths, legends and poetry.*
(South Eastern Education and Library Board)

## Educational

The stimulating atmosphere of many libraries encourages children from primary and secondary schools to turn to the library for homework and research purposes. Literacy and information skills are key to success across the range of life skills/experience, eg standards of behaviour, values as well as discrete skills. Access is given in many libraries to ICT for children who have no other access and where they feel safe and comfortable. Libraries have a key role in enabling children to access information and to find the things they are looking for, as well as to encourage reading for enjoyment so that children don't lose the creative side of their development. The public library is the only before and after form of learning support for reading:

*It is never too late in the library if you get chucked out of school – or indeed in later life.*

The educational value of libraries, relating to children and literacy and educational attainment, was highlighted as one of the key objectives by one inner London authority:

*The most important thing we do is work towards raising the standards of children's reading in the borough. It is one of our key objectives and it is a borough-wide priority.*

Again, from the estate in Northern Ireland, the educational role of libraries is high-lighted:

> *The role of the library has become more important as reading skills have suffered because of the time taken up by the Northern Ireland curriculum. We are increasingly filling the gap. Libraries also have a role in helping primary and pre-school children develop the higher reading skills of skimming, scanning, selecting what is relevant which are needed to use the technology fruitfully . . . A book can take you somewhere else, and that's specially important for children from this environment.* (South Eastern Education and Library Board)

One chief librarian quoted Isaac Asimov's experience of libraries as a useful reminder of the role of libraries in the educational process:

> I received the fundamentals of my education in school, but that was not enough. My real education, the superstructure, the details, the true architecture, I got out of the public library. For an impoverished child whose family could not afford books, the library was the open door to wonder and achievement, and I can never be sufficiently grateful that I had the wit to charge through that door and make the most of it.

## Support for literacy

Although traditionally, a central tenet of the British public library service has been the importance of supporting reading and literacy, there has been little in the professional literature to indicate how libraries might define 'literacy' or what types of literacy they might actively support. The research discovered that there was uniform agreement amongst library authorities to support reading literacy, placing particular importance on the pre-school years as providing a fundamental base for later literacy. However, there was an ambivalence about libraries' support for the formal reading process in terms of inculcating specific reading skills. There was, though, significant support for information skills development, which could be seen as having a significant reading component. The majority of authorities thought that formal reading was the remit of schools, with great importance attached to the libraries' role in fostering recreational reading and in instilling the desire to read. Southwark, in particular, emphasized the importance of encouraging literacy in all children – an issue of considerable importance with teenagers in the borough.

Much of the evidence collected concentrated on reading literacy, with scant attention given to the new literacies: a generic term used for the other types of literacy – visual, graphic and computer-oriented, and acknowledging that the process of reading extends beyond the printed word to encompass decoding of visual and non-linear forms.

## Reading development

An Arts Council for Scotland promotion proposed:

Every child a reading child.
Every adult a reading adult.

This seems a good message to sum up the results of the Place for Children research, from the perspective of parents and teachers asked about the value of the library in their child's reading development. They overwhelmingly indicated that they saw libraries as key supporters of children's reading. The message that reading is not just about reading scheme performance or performance in school, but something children can do for fun and outside the formal educational framework, was foremost in people's thinking. Thus, giving children access to a variety of reading materials, particularly when they had few, if any, books in the home environment, was invaluable.

Public libraries were seen as the driving force for children's reading development from the earliest ages, able to forge the kinds of partnerships with parents which no other institution was able to do. Promoting children's reading was amongst many libraries' highest priorities, on the grounds that 'if they got it wrong for children they got it wrong for everyone.' Knowing someone else who loves books is the most important factor:

*We are enriching children's lives by fostering a love of reading, a love of learning and curiosity about life.*

*Choosing is fun, reading is fun, books are adventures.*

Children need to succeed in the reading process. The public library was regularly seen as the agency to stimulate enthusiasm and passion for reading, with teachers and parents, as well as librarians, acknowledging that the enrichment of fiction meant a great deal to children and adults too:

*The trick of reading, because it's fun, is what they learn from libraries. We can help parents who would be intimidated going into school to ask what to get their children.*

It was seen as impossible to measure the effect of someone reading a book because the impact might be far-reaching in emotional, social or intellectual terms. The sharing of a story in groups and personally broadens children and offers them a window into other things, reinforcing their own experiences, fears, enjoyment. Children experiencing a story also develop an awareness of language, rhythms. Socially it builds confidence and understanding of other people's situations. This impact, of course, may not be felt until much later in an individual's life.

Libraries offer a model of adult and child sharing the enjoyment of books. That was viewed as important to parents as well as to children: to imitate other readers who model all kinds of reading. Not only were children learning how to behave in a public place such as the library, but they were becoming familiar with different types of reading, such as quiet reading for study, browsing, reading to each other. This has the advantage of showing them that all sorts of people do read. In addition, children learn to interact with people outside the defined roles of family or school and develop relationships, for which there are no particular models.

The public library reinforces what takes place in schools, by developing favourable attitudes to books and creating a reading environment. It was also seen by parents as an excellent means of exposing children to a wider range of more advanced reading material than most schools would provide.

## Reading trails

Reading trails in a number of libraries were seen as a good way of promoting literature. These tended to cover fiction and often poetry, but non-fiction reading trails had appealed particularly to children less interested in fiction. After a summer reading promotion in one authority, a survey of teachers showed that 63% of teachers felt that children had progressed more in their reading than they would have expected:

> *The whole point about the summer reading promotion is that it keeps children reading for those six weeks and . . . if they don't practise those skills and they don't keep reading, then they go back to school in September and they've fallen behind.*

## Support for parents

It is clear from the research that the library is an enormously important resource for parents: an organization which can empower parents. Parents can be helped to have the courage and the background knowledge of what they can achieve simply by reading, talking and listening with their children. Several libraries noted the value of helping the parent and supporting them no matter how poor their literacy skills were – making them aware that they do, and can, have a significant impact in developing their children's reading. Parents need to be educated about what their children like to read, and encouraged to make use of the library because often they do not know where to start. This is particularly important for children without a family reading background. On the whole, the people who did not join their children to the library in many areas were the parents who were scared of libraries, because they were unfamiliar with them and maybe did not know that borrowing books was free.

Some parents clearly thought that all their children's learning should be done at school, and took little or no responsibility for homework or reading with their children, so again this was a group where some education or support was needed. On the whole, though, parents were already asking libraries for more support for their children's reading. This was seen as a high priority for many libraries, whether informally within the library, talking to groups, or working with mothers on storytelling techniques – extending and developing their skills informally – and linking to nurseries. Initiatives such as the Bookstart projects were seen as significant in their support for parents, too. A number of librarians emphasized this:

> *Librarians not only read to children but model book-sharing for parents. Saturdays, the men bring in the kiddies and blether, while the kids play with the toys and borrow books.*

> *We promote reading through guidance to parents and children. The most effective activities are book talks. I go into schools with a carpet bag: I read extracts. But to allow this to happen, you have to have a system which allows staff to gain this knowledge. Libraries and literacy go together automatically. Perhaps we need a poster campaign linking the two.*

Parents themselves recognized the value of access to a wide variety of books:

> *. . . free access to large numbers of books extends my choice, and it doesn't matter so much if we choose a book and don't like it. I value libraries for the scope to make mistakes and different choices.*

Edinburgh's provision of toys was seen as helpful for the under-fives, because parents could leave their children happily occupied while they chose their own books, thus providing a support for parents' reading development, too.

Birmingham libraries talked about their work with a self-help group for parents of children with special needs. Also, a member of staff who was deaf told stories at a local school for deaf children. The information bureau in Birmingham central children's library, the Centre for the Child, provided reading for parents to enable them to support and develop their children themselves, in a way that benefitted the child and the family. Birmingham had also piloted a project with ethnic minority parents of pre-school children. Their Brightstart research into literacy in two areas of the city showed that one of the barriers was that parents did not think that black children and parents were welcome in the library. That was partly because of lack of confidence in using libraries but such parents really wanted libraries to be more explicit about welcoming all children.

Other barriers included a fear of damaging books and fines, although many libraries do not charge fines for under-fives or children with a disability under 16. The North Eastern Education and Library Board (Northern Ireland) had a Read to Succeed scheme for parents and carers through local initiatives in further and higher education, teaching parents how to help their children's reading. The Board was bidding for Peace and Reconciliation funding for paired reading schemes.

## Family literacy groups

Family literacy groups have also become more common in libraries, with an emphasis on the importance of sharing books with children from an early age and often specifically targeting parents whose own reading is weak. Many children who have literacy problems have parents with literacy problems. However, most parents with very poor literacy want better for their children. Libraries need to be part of family literacy schemes, particularly in terms of the long-term progress of adults, offering support after literacy schemes have finished. A family literacy project in one authority was linked closely to a City and Guilds qualification in wordpower.

## Family reading groups

Family reading groups in libraries were shown to have really benefitted children's development. Children who would not normally speak up in groups became quite happy to talk about the books they liked to read in front of a group of people. In supporting family reading and family literacy, the library provides a context which is non threatening and non-judgmental: 'It is about helping the parent and supporting them no matter how poor their literacy skills are.' A survey of the Family Library Link undertaken in one authority, to see how families used the library, demonstrated the value of having soft sitting areas, where parents and children could sit together.

Hampshire summed up this whole area well:

> By providing the widest range of good children's literature, by promoting reading and libraries. For pre-schoolers, promoting the library to parents also. Through storytimes, we help children's language development and social skills, and involve parents in the experience. Storytelling is probably the most under-rated and best activity we organise. The contact for children of non-articulate parents may be even more important than for children of well-educated parents. (Hampshire)

## Services

Library authorities throughout the UK were shown to be providing a rapidly changing variety of initiatives and activities for children and young people. In a number of authorities, the public library was seen as the driving force for children's reading development and seen as the main justification for having a well-developed children's library service. Often, this had started with the Bookstart projects, supplying books to babies through health centres and clinics. Most authorities offered holiday events for children as well as exciting up-to-date collections of books, magazines, audio cassettes. Increasing numbers of libraries were also providing ICT for children, with access to the Internet, CD-ROMs and basic software. Some authorities were beginning to lend CD-ROMs for home use. The research identified some inspirational ideas, a few of which are highlighted below:

1   Birmingham had a children's mobile, called Words on Wheels, which was an exhibition collection taken out to under-fives groups, nurseries and shopping centres.

2   Hampshire had an early years project, with a dedicated vehicle which visited playgroups, mother and toddler groups, clinics, bed and breakfast hostels, making 4–5 visits per day, telling stories in clinic waiting rooms:

*We see differences in children over a 2–3 year period of use: in attention span, in knowledge of authors, in selection skills.* (Hampshire)

3   Northamptonshire had a bookbus, operating throughout the year, which travelled to playschemes for children with disabilities and to children in rural areas. It stopped for two hours with special needs children and thirty minutes with others. It was seen as a key to promoting enjoyment of reading.

4   Hampshire's literature festival had covered adults and children. In 1998, the Wessex Book Fair had 10,000 visitors.

5   Leeds City Voice Festival in 1998 had a 'beautiful' commingling of adult and children's events.

6   Southwark had recently set up a teenage reading group, to emphasize the value of reading and improving reading and literacy standards. Observation of a teenage reading group session during the research showed an almost wholly unstructured session which clearly worked wonderfully well, with the teenagers appearing comfortable, well motivated and at ease with the library staff. During the session, plenty of books, including paperbacks and graphic novels, and magazines were looked at, discussed and recommended to friends and school mates: personal peer recommendations were clearly important, although the staff were consulted, too.

7   Northamptonshire had developed a homework help club, called the information zone, which aimed to support children's real needs as well as the National Curriculum, through self-study. This had developed from more standard homework collections, and there were plans to offer e-mail links to a homework librarian in libraries where a homework club was not feasible.

8   Leeds had appointed learning librarians in the inner city in very high-tech learning centres in five libraries and four high schools. They thought that all librarians would become learning librarians in the near future – an extension of their traditional role, but needing to be much more high-profile.

## Children's librarians

Linked to all of the above was evidence of inspired, knowledgeable and highly motivated children's librarians working in different authorities and many different environments – all impressive in their commitment to bettering the lot of children. Library staff, parents and teachers recognized the prime importance of libraries in providing a wide range of books and other materials. Access to those materials and the nurturing role of knowledgeable librarians in fostering a love of reading were seen as vital to the development of the growing child, as was the value of librarians modelling good reading behaviour. A number of teachers saw librarians as very knowledgeable and able to introduce books, spread enthusiasm, give them something to take back to their own classrooms. Teachers were generally seen to have a relatively limited knowledge of modern authors. Thus, librarians became even more important in offering children wide choice and opportunity to explore new authors. Librarians got to know children informally and that helped them to choose the right book for the child at the time:

> *We connect the book to a child. We act as a two-way channel because we feed back the views and thoughts and responses of children to the book makers, authors and publishers. We bring in new material and make sure the child's diet is a rich one.*

> *. . . two-way relationship, a feeling of trust builds up, as children realise there's someone here who is interested in them. We put ourselves out for children and that gives them a good feeling.*

There was clearly a tension in some authorities between a large central team of specialist children's librarians and direct local service delivery; central advisory work and grass-roots delivery. This was a particular challenge, because parents and teachers wanted to see specialists available locally and this created a tension at management level in terms of how best to deploy specialist staff. Other authorities thought that it was not necessary for everyone to be children's specialists, merely to ensure that all staff were aware of children's needs.

But, despite all of this evidence of good practice, there was still a distinct and maybe surprising lack of confidence amongst librarians in the value of what they were doing:

> *We're making a really major contribution to literacy development yet somehow there's a lack of confidence that what we're doing is worth sharing.*

## Training

The amount of training that had been received by librarians interviewed varied enormously, as did the interest in the need for training either to improve skills or to keep abreast of new developments. Similarly, whether or not there was training available within the authority varied considerably from authority to authority, as did access to training offered through, for example, the Library Association and the Youth Libraries Group. There was evidence that the more training that had been received and was available, the more individuals perceived the need for more training! Northamptonshire was planning a well-structured training programme, with modules on working with children. Several authorities noted that their regular meetings to review children's books, as part of the book selection process, was a vital part of training and expanding knowledge of children's books and children's reading needs, as was participation in the annual Carnegie/Kate Greenaway nominations.

There was strong support for experience as a necessary element of preparing librarians to work with children:

*My experience as a mother has been helpful.*

Personality, attitude, enthusiasm and honesty were seen as crucial:

*Flexibility and integrity are much more important than any training you could get.*

## Collection development

One of the most important responsibilities of the librarian is often taken to be that of planning, building, maintaining and promoting a dynamic and pertinent collection.

Collection development involves not only the selection of new stock but also collection evaluation and review, preservation, conservation and the promotion of collections. Generally it is assumed that a written policy statement is critical for the successful development of a collection. The research indicated that half of the respondents possessed a written collection policy, but when library authorities were asked whether they had established a specific collection policy that addressed children's reading, only 8% of respondents indicated that they possessed such a policy. Consideration of children's reading might well be encompassed within a general written policy statement, but there is some concern here that this has not been seen to be strategically important.

The most striking omission in policy statements was selection criteria for non-book materials and electronic resources. There was some evidence that such materials were now being taken more seriously, and the roll-out of the Public Library Network should act as a catalyst for further development in this field. However, it is high time that librarians were beginning to consider the specific selection requirements of electronic and non-book materials.

There has been little writing on the area of collection development in recent years and this study has furthered our understanding of the current scene. It has also highlighted a considerable dearth in statements of policy concerned with children's reading development and a woeful lack of attention being paid to anything other than the conventional book stock. This clearly has implications for the management and training of librarians, as well as for the future strategic direction of children's libraries.

## Stock management

Leeds libraries had recently developed a reader strategy to replace their stock development strategy and concentrate on readers:

> *We've thrown away our stock development strategy. If you get away from the business about whether you're supposed to be reading highbrow books or lowbrow books . . . if you get away from all the snobbery that surrounds reading and all the worthiness, and if instead you say 'We're not about books, we're about reading', then you can simultaneously cover people's leisure reading and their serious reading.* (Leeds)

Leeds libraries also have a clear view of the role of the library in the creation of readers for life:

> *The public library is about imaginative discovery . . . it's about creative discovery as a reading experience. Isn't it a shame that we lose our sense of crying out when we find a good book? I love it when a child discovers something and all those discoveries are new and are very special and they are the beginning of the reading journeys that will be life long and will go up and down and in and out and weave into a rich tapestry of the reader.* (Leeds)

## Performance measures

The perception that all public services should be accountable has grown steadily over the past two decades but little use of performance indicators other than issue figures and counting activities was found during the research. Honourable exceptions to this were Northamptonshire and Southwark:

> *There is no point in doing anything unless it has an outcome and it can be measured and it is going to contribute to moving something forward. We do not have the resources just to do things for the sake of it, so anything we do, we would measure and we would look at the value of what we are doing in terms of what measurement and in terms of what the customers say in terms of feedback to the service. And so it's critical; if you set objectives, you have to measure them . . . You have to know what you are measuring. Some things are quantitative, but you shouldn't knock the quantitative, because in some circumstances that is the absolute appropriate measurement. If you are looking at indications of performance in different ways, then you look at quality and you can look at it in a fairly hard-edged way by benchmarking and soft data. If you have a teenage reading group, what are you measuring, what is the objective of the group? Is it to get them to come into the library, is it to get them to read more proficiently, is it to get them to read other things than they would normally read in schools? All these things have to be defined before you can start the measurement. And that is all too often what people do not do . . . You don't just do something because you think it is a good thing to do. There has to be a reason for doing it . . . The objectives are the key to it.* (Northamptonshire)

*We have client–contractor arrangements with a whole monitoring regime to assess this, which includes all aspects of the children's service. It is also a major part of our business plan that we produce every year. It is an important element of how we operate. We have a specification which includes what things we should be doing and the standard to which they should be done and that is monitored . . . Performance indicators are dealing with inputs and outputs, how much you spend on staff, how much you spend on stock, how many libraries you have got . . . Then we measure the outputs, number of issues, number of visitors, number of children who attend sessions . . . It is important to know what you are doing and to know from the outset how you can measure something you are offering.*
(Southwark)

Southwark, though, pointed out that measuring can sometimes be counterproductive:

*With the homework clubs we are measuring the impact by asking parents, schools and the children themselves, but this can be counter-productive. Homework clubs are meant to be different from school. If you then try to measure it all in terms of improvement of academic performance, it becomes just another area where children are assessed when it is so important that they enjoy the experience.*

*But the outcomes, the benefit that everyone gets from them . . . that is probably long-term. You have children in the under-5s session. How do you measure the impact of that and when does it show? It is very hard to say we do that and the end result is that ten years later this person gets 5 As at GCSE level.*

There was a general agreement with this view that measuring long-term outcomes was difficult and little use was made of output measures:

*How do you measure the impact of storytelling? So far our evaluation is largely anecdotal, looking at the reaction of parents and children . . . for example, family reading groups which everyone seems to enjoy. This is very hard to quantify. How do you measure whether children are happier since they've started the group, whether you have made an impact on their lives?*

In particular, it was felt that there were no adequate formal measures for reading development, because libraries were in no position to assess children's reading. The actual measurement of reading and reading skills could only go on in schools. Many librarians measured success almost in kind:

*You can tell how happy the customers are just by blethering to them.*

*When the front door opens and I see this torpedo come through the doors and pick up a book – that is success, or a child cries when it is time to leave.*

*Dealing with school visits, reluctant and less able readers – you're a bit like an unprimed bomb.*

Seeing notes in local newspapers of children's achievements, and remembering them as library members, was noted as one method of evaluating impact. Political awareness was highlighted as an important indicator in terms of giving politicians a feel for value and impact:

*People have a good opinion of us – but how to improve the impact was a problem . . . the library is not just a book service – it is the Council presence in the community. Politicians will only rate us if they see us as useful to them.*

Hampshire said we could ask parents:

*'Do you think your children's reading has improved because of the library?', but that's making the library too much like school and implying a single-track view of its function. Our measures include issues, class visits and activities and staff enthusiasm. Staff are not enthusiastic if they're not getting a positive response from the public.*

The South East London Performance Indicators Group (cross-borough) was looking at benchmarking, including children's services, on the basis that benchmarking can show that one authority is better than others, or can be a means of asking questions, a different way of looking at service standards. However, Hampshire acknowledged the problems of finding comparisons:

*We don't find bench-marking useful, and, in any case, that doesn't measure impact. No other author-ity is really similar to us, Essex has 100 service points, we have 54. Our territory is completely different from Kent or Lancashire, and so are our reader expectations. We have a demanding public who would soon tell us if we were failing to provide a service of high quality. The only way you can prove a service is having impact is if people return, and they do here. Each year we do a profession-al audit, going to all professional staff, asking what we should report to members. Again and again, the audit shows the importance of family visits on Saturdays and of children's services overall.*

A number of authorities were intending to introduce the CIPFA standard children's survey but it was too early for anyone to have had experience of this.

Overall, it was felt that the questions that mattered were: Was visiting the library a good experience? Did my child get what s/he needed? The responses maybe are not quantifiable, because the experiences are ongoing.

## Partnerships

Networks of contacts were seen as crucial to ensure that libraries were not inward-looking and were responding to new or forthcoming initiatives at local as well as national levels, and ensuring that libraries remained on the local authority's agenda.

Local government reorganization in some authorities had enabled more collaboration between departments and more integrated strategies. But in Wales, where authorities had just resurfaced from a major local government reorganization, there were concerns about the erosion of the children's librarianship specialism. In some authorities, there was considerable pride in independence since local government reorganization. This threatened links with the former parent county but also strengthened links within the borough, eg with education, social sciences, arts departments.

## Corporate

In Edinburgh, services for children and young people were seen as key in the city services strategy, with the education department as the lead department in this strategic push. There were key links to other service areas, through the chief executives' support groups and corporate information strategy, giving the library service to children a high council profile. In Birmingham, after the beginning of the Birmingham Year of Reading, a cross-departmental reading group had been established with representatives from education, community education, business partnerships and libraries, who were developing a strategic approach to reading as part of the city's lifelong learning strategy.

## Education

Education departments were working in many areas of potential overlap with libraries, such as promoting reading, combating illiteracy, and developing information skills, but some librarians were concerned:

*We would love to be in on the planning, but it hasn't happened.*

*Initially we were horrified how little the education department had considered the role of libraries.*

Links with the schools library services across the UK were variable and sometimes strained. Increasingly, they have distinct but complementary roles, and a number of authorities had clearly defined policy documents outlining the responsibilities of each department. The People's Network and the National Grid for Learning make liaison with Education increasingly necessary.

## Health

In Birmingham, the family literacy strategy had developed a relationship between libraries and the health authorities. It was seen as difficult to keep promoting literacy when there was so much poverty and particularly infant mortality. By working more closely with health visitors, through the Bookstart project, it had become clear that literacy was relevant, and a crucial part of child development which health workers should be involved in.

## Youth

One authority, recognizing the problem of children who can read but don't, particularly boys, was beginning to work with the play and youth services.

## Social services

Northamptonshire worked with their local social services department, developing a scheme called A Book for your Child, which was about children in residential homes or care.

## Conclusions

The research highlighted some wonderful work being undertaken in libraries. It found evidence throughout the UK of how libraries and librarians contribute to children's reading development to a degree which has never been identified before. Excellent examples had been found of how work with pre-school children, reluctant readers, special needs children, home-educated children and teenagers had improved reading skills, helped to socialize children and provided a secure environment. In addition, the role of libraries was highlighted in supporting parents' own reading and helping them gain confidence with their own children. The library was highlighted as a social, educational, cultural centre, at the heart of many communities. This role appears undiminished and, in many senses, is growing as we head towards the millennium. The uses of technology to support children's reading and skills development have not yet been fully explored by libraries, but the development of the Public Library Network and the National Grid for Learning provide the imminent opportunity for libraries to grasp this potential.

However, there were some negatives, too:

1  Libraries appeared not to be making as much use of national or regional literacy initiatives as they might have been.
2  Some public libraries did not see literacy and formal reading support as an essential part of their service provision. Maybe a redefinition of literacy and the role of libraries is required.
3  There appeared to be little support for the literacy of children with special needs and multicultural literacy. This was a cause for concern.
4  There was a lack of strategic planning and integration of purpose and outcome, linked with systematic monitoring. Only 30% of authorities had a policy statement

for service to children and young people, and only 26% had promotional policies.

5 There was a lack of cohesive policies to support reading development: a clear ethos is needed within authorities which regards reading development as a prime role.

6 Children's librarians were often not seizing the opportunities offered by corporate policies running across departmental boundaries.

7 There was an absence of policies on Internet access and provision for children, and a general lack of multimedia aids.

8 There was a need for policies and knowledge/skills to help the selection of appropriate ICT products, particularly to support reading. There was considerable lack of understanding of the potential which ICT could provide to support reading development. This needs urgent remedies.

9 There was very little local research being done beyond pure collection of statistics, and little understanding of, let alone sharing of, research into any aspect of children's library provision or library contribution to reading development, social inclusion, cultural, recreational, educational development.

10 The importance of parents in children's reading development was readily acknowledged by librarians, but the difficulty of reaching parents was rarely overcome.

11 The importance of reaching teenagers was generally acknowledged, but only rarely borne out in service provision.

12 The value for special needs children of all kinds of a supportive library environment was clearly recognized but only limited evidence of implementation of effective services was found.

13 Local government reorganization had brought into being many smaller authorities with the concomitant problem of new heads of service, in many cases with a significant knowledge gap.

14 There were clearly significant differences in the quality of children's library provision between top and bottom authorities. Major differences in provision and the absence of any national standards were apparent.

15 The goodwill and enthusiasm of staff were often eroded by budget constraints, changing structures and reorganization, both internal and as a result of central government policies.

16 Little attention was being given to new literacies or oral literacy, particularly amongst ethnic minorities.

## Further research

Inevitably research for A Place for Children identified areas where further research is needed – some of it fairly urgently. The most critical areas where research funding would aid children's reading and provide real evidence to underpin children's library service developments are:

- longitudinal studies of children's reading
- impact studies of libraries on children's reading and research to demonstrate an improvement in reading age after attendance at library activities
- study of why support for special needs, beyond children with physical and visual impairment, appears to be limited to a few key authorities only
- study of the poor take-up of ICT in children's libraries, with demonstration projects or examples of good practice
- effects of the decline in the number of professional staff on children's reading and the use of libraries
- work to counteract the limitations of qualitative measures and indicators which could be used politically.

# A Place for Children research

## Research project and methodology

The project was funded by the British Library Research and Innovation Centre, and ran from November 1996 until June 1998. It was conceived as a collaborative piece of research by the principal institutions teaching and researching in the field of children's library provision, and drew on expertise within three British universities: the University of Central England in Birmingham; Loughborough University; and the University of Wales, Aberystwyth.

## Project aims

A nationwide study was decided on, to include not only the collection of data through the most searching questionnaire survey of children's services ever undertaken, but also in-depth case studies from every part of the UK. Comprehensive literature searches were also undertaken. There were three core questions asked by the researchers:

- How do public libraries benefit children?
- What makes for an effective service?
- How do public libraries define and assess success?

The research priorities of the British Library Research and Innovation Centre at the time when A Place for Children study was proposed were focused on users, public library provision, and value and impact. Those research issues we had identified were therefore clearly in line with national policy on library development. It was essential to refine the issues into specific objectives that would link with policy needs and the practicality of developing library services for children and young people. The study was intended to produce results that would have a direct impact on managing services.

## Project objectives

Seven objectives were set by the project team:

1   To identify and collate existing data. As has been indicated in the introduction to this work, there have been many studies relevant to children's reading and a few on children's libraries, but none of them on their own have provided sufficient analytical depth to influence policy-makers effectively on the role of libraries in children's reading, or enable library managers to move services forward. We needed to bring these together, collect and compare their findings, and assess them against our own findings.

2   To investigate the range of services and activities being delivered. The LISU surveys had provided baseline data and there was need now to develop the qualitative aspects of that statistical work to explain further what was happening and why. From this work we could then identify recommendations for future action. A comprehensive questionnaire survey of all library authorities in England and Wales, with a 75.8% overall response rate, yielded much rich data. The questionnaire was distributed with the annual LISU survey questionnaire. Close liaison with the LISU team enabled us to ensure there was no duplication of questions, but rather a development of the LISU data to provide a detailed picture of the service context, service purpose, clients, collection development, access, promotion, service assessment and service development.

3   To identify good practice in terms of initiatives to improve literacy. While the survey provided outline data on initiatives and practice across the UK, it was seen as essential to undertake detailed, in-depth case studies that would yield rich insights by enabling the research team to engage with librarians, teachers, parents/carers and children. Library authorities were selected partly on the basis of national, socio-geographical and sectoral balance, but also largely on the grounds of good practice.

4   To consider the contribution of the new literacies which embrace a wide range of media. The relationship between the new media and children's reading development is now recognized to be important (Lonsdale, 1996), and it was seen as essential to understand how libraries were responding to this, through both the survey and the case study investigations. Were children's wider literacy needs being supported?

5   To define criteria for excellence in service delivery in the UK. Documentation from library authorities, including policy statements, was another rich source of infor-

mation that, together with the interview and questionnaire data, enabled us to identify best practice criteria. Nationally applicable standards for services were not seen as a useful goal – the view also of the LISC(E) Working Party, (Library and Information Services Council, 1995, 49). We were intent rather on identifying the critical success factors for quality services to children and young people.

6    To identify appropriate output measures. While there were readily available quantitative measures of effectiveness, we were interested in how services measured their impact on children's reading development and what recommendations we could offer in this complex area.

7    To provide recommendations for action by relevant parties. These would include policy-makers at national, regional and local levels, librarians, teachers and the book trade.

## Project management

Project directors were: Professor Judith Elkin, University of Central England (UCE) in Birmingham; Professor Margaret Kinnell Evans, Loughborough University; and Ray Lonsdale, Senior Lecturer at the University of Wales, Aberystwyth. Project coordination was undertaken by: Debbie Denham, Senior Lecturer at UCE; Peggy Heeks, Research Fellow at Loughborough University; and Chris Armstrong, Researcher at the University of Wales, Aberystwyth; with fellow researchers, Roger Fenton from Aberystwyth and Karin Richter, UCE. Together, the project team offered considerable experience of both practice and research in children's librarianship and literature, as well as in the wider field of organizational management. Claire Creaser of the Library and Information Statistics Unit, Loughborough University, supported the statistical analysis in the later stages of the project, and also contributed her wide experience of children's library statistics from the LISU Surveys of Library Services to Schools and Children. There are now nine of these annual reports, the latest of which was published in November 1998 (Creaser and Murphy, 1998), and this has enabled LISU to provide evidence of trends in library provision for children across the UK.

## Advisory group

An advisory group was formed at the beginning of the project to support and monitor the design of the project, including the research tools, and to foster liaison with library authorities, the education sector and the book trade. The members were:

| | |
|---|---|
| Wendy Cooling | Freelance Consultant |
| Isobel Thompson | Project Manager, British Library Research and Innovation Centre |
| Kimberley Reynolds | Reader in Children's Literature, Roehampton Institute |

| John Dunne | Assistant County Librarian, Hampshire County Libraries |
| Alec Williams | Head of Children's Services, Leeds City Library Service |
| Anne Everall | Manager, Centre for the Child, Birmingham City Library Service |
| Philip Marshall | Principal Libraries Officer (Client Services), Nottinghamshire County Libraries |
| Pearl Valentine | Chief Librarian, North Eastern Education and Library Board. |

## Research methods

Research methods included: a critical assessment of the literature; consultation with relevant agencies; a questionnaire survey of library authorities to determine current services and attitudes; and a series of case studies and focus groups to examine the perception of service provision held by librarians, teachers, parents and carers, and children and young people.

## Literature review

A literature search was carried out to identify relevant key texts and gaps in the literature. LISA and ERIC were the most relevant databases and these were searched to include materials from 1990 onwards. Keywords used to search these databases included: children's reading and libraries; reading development; reading promotion; literacy promotion; and reading surveys. Other keywords focused on performance indicators and performance measures. The search was also limited by searching for material which discussed children in the 0-to-16 age range.

The literature indicated that there were very few recent books on children's librarianship in the UK. *Focus on the child* by Elkin and Lonsdale (1996) was the major monograph about children's libraries produced in the UK in the last 20 years. Much of the other material noted was ephemeral in nature and largely produced in the USA and Canada. The majority of this literature concentrated on reading in schools and therefore was not of direct relevance to this research project. It became evident that little had been done to offer qualitative evaluation of the impact the public library has, particularly in the area of children's reading. The analysis of the literature brought together relevant existing data; unpublished reports identified through networking; and statistical data from LISU. It also raised many questions about appropriate mechanisms for measuring impact.

## Questionnaire survey

A questionnaire survey of all UK library authorities was undertaken to identify:

- current services and activities, including reading promotion activities, IT-based services and access, user education, targeted information services
- librarians' perceptions of the major issues facing services in developing access and use to meet the reading needs of children and young people.

Further documentation, such as strategic plans, policy documents and marketing material, was requested. This supplementary documentation was used to support the case studies. The questionnaire was relatively long and contained detailed questions which required judgements to be made about the value of various aspects of service provision as well as questions which requested information on current provision. It was sent to the heads of children's services in all UK library authorities. A 75% response rate was achieved, indicating the importance which the respondents attached to this area of research.

## Case studies

To supplement the questionnaire survey, a number of detailed case studies in library authorities throughout the UK were undertaken. These authorities were selected using a number of criteria, including the need to provide a national balance and to select authorities which would provide examples of good practice in the development and support of children's reading skills. There was a concern to cover a wide range of social and geographical environments, taking into account both rural and inner-city situations, ethnic and cultural minority language needs, and differing organizational structures.

Initial funding for the project allowed for eight case studies. The research team and the advisory group strongly felt that this was not sufficient, so bids were prepared to obtain extra funds. LISC(NI) provided finance for a further case study in Northern Ireland, and a supplementary grant from BLRIC enabled three further case studies to be planned in England. The research team in Wales was able to undertake two further case studies within the budget already allocated.

The work within the case studies was intensive, ensuring that a wide spread of data was collected. While a range of socio-economic factors has been shown to influence children's reading, the emphasis in this study lay with the role of the public library rather than with the numerous additional variables. Issues which had emerged in the literature, from the experience of the team and the advisory group and through the initial analysis of the questionnaire survey, were explored. Interviews were identified as the most relevant methodology to be used with library staff. Key personnel to be interviewed in each authority were identified as: head of the library service; head of children's service; professional and paraprofessional staff. The core questions identified in the project aims provided the basis for the interview questions. These were also used to survey teachers and parents/carers in a series of focus-group sessions. Children and young people were observed using the library, and informal discussion groups were set up with children. The movement of children around the library and their selection of materials were observed. Questions asked of children centred on their use of libraries and choice of materials.

The authorities which participated were:

- *England*
  - Birmingham
  - Leeds
  - Northampton
  - Hampshire (and Southampton)
  - Southwark
  - Croydon
- *Northern Ireland*
  - North Eastern Education and Library Board (NEELB)
  - South Eastern Education and Library Board (SEELB)
- *Scotland*
  - Edinburgh
  - Stirling
- *Wales*
  - Neath and Port Talbot
  - Ceredigion
  - Ynys Môn

## Dissemination

Dissemination was identified early on as of overriding importance for this research. The project was perceived as having national significance and relevance, and so its progress and the final results were disseminated as widely as possible throughout the library and information profession.

Dissemination methods included:

- an interim report which provides information on the progress of the project
- this monograph
- articles in relevant professional and scholarly journals, both national and international, in the national press and other media
- a one-day conference for the library profession
- presentations to other relevant conferences.

## References

Creaser, C and Murphy, A (1998) *A survey of library services to schools and children in the UK 1997–8*, Loughborough Library and Information Statistics Unit.

Elkin, J and Lonsdale, R (1996) *Focus on the child: libraries, literacy and learning*, Library Association Publishing.

Library and Information Services Council (England) Working Party on Library Services for Children and Young People (1995) *Investing in children: the future of library services for children and young people*, Library Information Series 22, HMSO.

Lonsdale, R (1996) Media and the child. In Elkin, J and Lonsdale, R, *Focus on the child: libraries, literacy and learning*, Library Association Publishing.

# Statistical summary and analysis

Prepared for the Place for Children project by Claire Creaser, CStat, Library and Information Statistics Unit, Loughborough University.

## Contents

## Introduction

The tables and graphs presented in this report are intended to give a descriptive summary of the data collected by the Place for Children project in 1997. No comment or interpretation of the findings has been included, except in so far as this is necessary to the understanding of the data presented. Results are presented in the order of the questionnaire, and labelling for each item is derived from the wording on the questionnaire, where more detail is to be found.

A number of different formats have been used, as appropriate to each item. In each case, the averages – either average ratings or percentages of respondents ticking an item – for the English counties, metropolitan districts, unitary authorities, London, Wales, Scotland and Northern Ireland have been given separately (where there are sufficient data). The total for the whole of the UK has been given for comparison purposes. Distributions have not been included. Factor analyses have been carried out on the rating questions, and summary results are presented.

## Notes on factor analysis

Factor analysis is a statistical technique which attempts to extract any underlying themes from the responses where a number of statements are rated on an ordinal scale. Its aim is to reduce a large number of individual statements to a much smaller number of indicators, called factors, each of which comprises a weighted average of the responses to each of the statements. Those statements which have the largest weights make the greatest contribution to the factor, and can be used to define it. Which these are depends entirely on the responses to the questionnaire, and in some instances seemingly unrelated items are combined into a single factor.

Factors are extracted, and presented here, in the order of their contribution to the overall variability in the data. Each factor can then be considered as a new variable, with values calculated for each of the respondents with complete data. These calculated values, called factor scores, can then be analysed in relation to other data available. In this report, where appropriate, average factor scores have been calculated for each of the sectors listed above, and those which are particularly high or low have been noted.

## Response rate

|  | Number of respondents | Response rate, % | % of population represented |
|---|---|---|---|
| Counties | 23 | 65.7 | 69.9 |
| Metropolitan districts | 25 | 69.4 | 74.8 |
| London | 26 | 78.8 | 79.7 |
| Unitary authorities | 19 | 70.4 | 65.8 |
| Wales | 21 | 95.5 | 91.8 |
| Scotland | 26 | 81.3 | 90.0 |
| NI | 4 | 80.0 | 83.5 |
| UK | 144 | 75.8 | 75.5 |

The percentages of the population represented by the responding authorities are based on total resident population, as figures for child populations are not yet available for all the new unitary authorities.

## Service context

Q 5  Percentage of library services operating schools library services

|  | % | Number of respondents |
|---|---|---|
| Counties | 82 | 22 |
| Metropolitan districts | 60 | 25 |
| London | 50 | 26 |
| Unitary authorities | 42 | 19 |
| Wales | 48 | 21 |
| Scotland | 40 | 25 |
| NI | 100 | 4 |
| UK | 55 | 142 |

### Q 6  Percentage of library services with specialist professional children's staff

|  | % | Number of respondents |
|---|---|---|
| Counties | 83 | 23 |
| Metropolitan districts | 60 | 25 |
| London | 77 | 26 |
| Unitary authorities | 68 | 19 |
| Wales | 38 | 21 |
| Scotland | 54 | 28 |
| NI | 50 | 4 |
| UK | 63 | 146 |

## Service purpose

### Q 7 & 8  Policy documents

|  | % with policy documents for | | | |
|---|---|---|---|---|
|  | Children's service | Number of respondents | Literacy | Number of respondents |
| Counties | 70 | 23 | 13 | 23 |
| Metropolitan districts | 29 | 24 | 16 | 25 |
| London | 19 | 26 | 4 | 26 |
| Unitary authorities | 26 | 19 | 16 | 19 |
| Wales | 43 | 21 | 5 | 21 |
| Scotland | 4 | 27 | 4 | 27 |
| NI | 25 | 4 | 0 | 4 |
| UK | 31 | 144 | 9 | 145 |

### Q 9 & 10  Service agreements/charters

|  | % with service agreement/charter for | | | |
|---|---|---|---|---|
|  | Parents | Number of respondents | Children | Number of respondents |
| Counties | 4 | 23 | 9 | 23 |
| Metropolitan districts | 4 | 24 | 4 | 24 |
| London | 12 | 26 | 8 | 26 |
| Unitary authorities | 5 | 19 | 0 | 19 |
| Wales | 5 | 21 | 5 | 21 |
| Scotland | 0 | 27 | 0 | 27 |
| NI | 50 | 4 | 25 | 4 |
| UK | 6 | 144 | 5 | 144 |

## Q 11    Importance of literacy

| | Average importance rating | | | | % of services which reflect the view | | | | Number of respondents |
|---|---|---|---|---|---|---|---|---|---|
| | Reading | Graphic | Visual | Other | Reading | Graphic | Visual | Other | |
| Counties | 5.0 | 3.7 | 3.7 | 4.3 | 100 | 78 | 73 | 48 | 22–3 |
| Metropolitan districts | 5.0 | 3.7 | 3.3 | 4.3 | 100 | 64 | 75 | 76 | 23–5 |
| London | 4.9 | 3.7 | 3.5 | 4.4 | 96 | 80 | 75 | 64 | 24–6 |
| Unitary authorities | 4.9 | 3.8 | 3.8 | 4.4 | 100 | 84 | 79 | 47 | 19 |
| Wales | 4.8 | 3.9 | 3.7 | 4.1 | 100 | 68 | 75 | 75 | 19–21 |
| Scotland | 4.9 | 3.4 | 3.5 | 3.8 | 100 | 86 | 96 | 52 | 27–8 |
| NI | 5.0 | 3.3 | 3.5 | 4.3 | 100 | 25 | 75 | 25 | 4 |
| UK | 4.9 | 3.7 | 3.5 | 4.2 | 99 | 76 | 79 | 59 | 138–46 |

A factor analysis was carried out on these data – with relatively little variation between authorities and only four items, a single factor was extracted.

## Q 12    Average importance rating of library functions

| | Provide inform-ation | Support education | Promote literacies | Promote reading | Inform-ation skills | Attract members | Instil desire | Provide access | Number of respondents |
|---|---|---|---|---|---|---|---|---|---|
| Counties | 4.9 | 4.0 | 4.7 | 4.7 | 4.4 | 4.7 | 4.9 | 4.9 | 23 |
| Metropolitan districts | 4.7 | 4.1 | 4.5 | 4.7 | 4.4 | 4.6 | 4.6 | 4.5 | 25 |
| London | 4.8 | 4.4 | 4.8 | 4.8 | 4.7 | 4.7 | 4.9 | 4.8 | 26 |
| Unitary authorities | 4.7 | 3.7 | 4.8 | 5.0 | 4.6 | 4.7 | 4.9 | 4.8 | 19 |
| Wales | 4.7 | 4.3 | 4.6 | 4.7 | 4.5 | 4.8 | 4.6 | 4.8 | 20–1 |
| Scotland | 4.9 | 4.0 | 4.8 | 4.9 | 4.7 | 4.8 | 4.9 | 4.8 | 28 |
| NI | 4.5 | 4.0 | 4.3 | 4.8 | 4.3 | 4.5 | 4.3 | 5.0 | 4 |
| UK | 4.8 | 4.1 | 4.7 | 4.8 | 4.5 | 4.7 | 4.8 | 4.8 | 145–6 |

A factor analysis was carried out on the responses to this question for the UK as a whole, and two factors were identified:

1   *Recreational* – low importance for support for education, high importance for promoting recreational reading, attracting members, instilling desire to read, and giving access to materials.

2  *Informational* – high importance for providing information, supporting formal education, promoting literacies and developing information skills; low importance for promotion of recreational reading.

Standardized factor scores for each of these aspects were calculated for all authorities, and the differences between the average scores in each sector examined. The graph in Figure A2.1 shows the relative positions of each authority on the two factors (there are likely to be points on the graph representing more than one authority). The average for the whole UK is at zero on both scales.

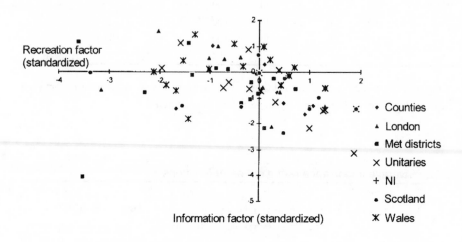

**Fig. A2.1**  *Recreational and informational factors*

Looking at the sector average, the metropolitan districts and Wales had below-average scores on the recreational factor (ie they rated the importance of these aspects below the UK average), whilst the English unitaries and Scotland had above-average scores on this measure (ie they rated the importance of these aspects more highly than the UK average). London and Wales scored above average on the information factor, with the unitaries below average.

## Clients

### Q 13 Library clients – average importance ratings

The graph in Figure A2.2 shows the average importance ratings in each sector on each item in the question.

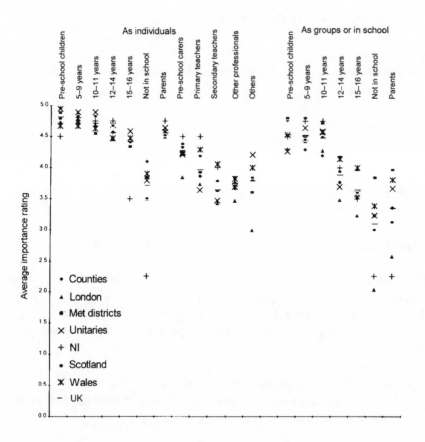

**Fig. A2.2**    *Library clients: average importance ratings*

Note: The ratings for the 'others' category are based on the following numbers of responses:

| | |
|---|---|
| Counties | 5 |
| Metropolitan districts | 5 |
| London | 3 |
| Unitary authorities | 5 |
| Wales | 3 |
| Scotland | 6 |
| Northern Ireland | 0 |
| UK | 27 |

Factor analysis of these items (excluding the 'others' category) extracted five factors, accounting for almost 80% of the variability in the data:

- *adults* as individuals
- *secondary* children in schools, children not in school as individuals and groups, parents as a group
- *schoolchildren* as individuals
- *primary* children in schools
- *pre-school* children as individuals and in groups.

The second of these factors is not well defined, and these categories seem to have little in common with each other. Looking at the average factor scores on each measure by sector, the following stand out:

1 English counties are below average on the *primary* factor, and above average on the *pre-school* factor.
2 The metropolitan districts are below average on the *schoolchildren* factor, and above average on the *second, mixed,* factor.
3 London is below average on the *second, mixed,* factor.
4 The English unitary authorities are above average on the *schoolchildren* factor.
5 Wales is above average on the *second, mixed* and *primary* factors, and below average on the *pre-school* factor.
6 Scotland is below average on the *second, mixed* factor.
7 Northern Ireland is above average on the *adult* and *primary* factors, and below average on the *second, mixed* and *pre-school* factors.

(Below-average factor scores indicate that the elements which are most important in that factor are rated as less important by that group on average than the average for the UK as a whole. Conversely, above-average factor scores indicate that the elements contributing most to those factors are rated as more important by that group than the average for the UK as a whole.)

### Q 14 Authority clients

Figure A2.3 shows percentages of authorities which consider these categories of user as clients:

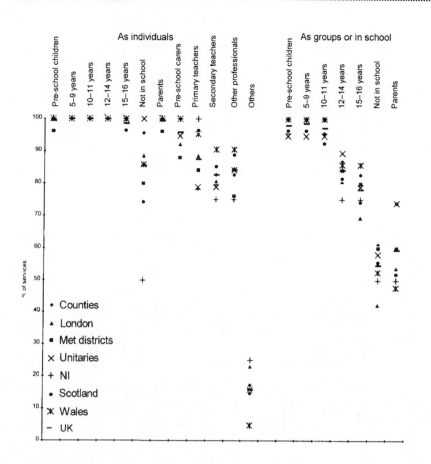

**Fig. A2.3**  *Authority clients*

## Q 15 Minority languages
### a) Welsh

|                                   | % of respondents |
|-----------------------------------|------------------|
| Spoken by children                | 76               |
| Spoken by children's librarians   | 57               |
| Used in storytelling etc.         | 71               |
| Used in library signs             | 81               |
| Actively added to collection      | 100              |

Results from a total of 21 authorities in Wales only. In addition, one English county and one London borough actively add Welsh material to their collections.

## b) Scottish Gaelic

| | % of respondents |
|---|---|
| Spoken by children | 15 |
| Spoken by children's librarians | 15 |
| Used in storytelling etc. | 7 |
| Used in library signs | 11 |
| Actively added to collection | 59 |

Results from a total of 27 authorities in Scotland only.

## c) Irish Gaelic

| | % of respondents |
|---|---|
| Spoken by children | 50 |
| Spoken by children's librarians | 25 |
| Used in storytelling etc. | 25 |
| Used in library signs | 25 |
| Actively added to collection | 75 |

Results from a total of four authorities in Northern Ireland only.

## Q 16 Targeted services/collections

Percentage of respondents with targeted services/collections for:

| | Reading difficulties | English as second language | Reluctant readers | Gifted children | Dyslexia | Blind/ partial sight | Other | Number of respondents |
|---|---|---|---|---|---|---|---|---|
| Counties | 39 | 61 | 48 | 13 | 30 | 83 | 4 | 23 |
| Metropolitan districts | 52 | 44 | 48 | 4 | 12 | 68 | 16 | 25 |
| London | 39 | 69 | 58 | 15 | 23 | 50 | 19 | 26 |
| Unitary authorities | 37 | 47 | 42 | 0 | 11 | 74 | 5 | 19 |
| Wales | 25 | 20 | 45 | 5 | 10 | 60 | 10 | 20 |
| Scotland | 46 | 35 | 54 | 15 | 27 | 62 | 12 | 26 |
| NI | 75 | 0 | 75 | 0 | 25 | 75 | 0 | 4 |
| UK | 41 | 46 | 50 | 9 | 20 | 66 | 11 | 143 |

## Q 17 & 18 Percentage of children who are library members

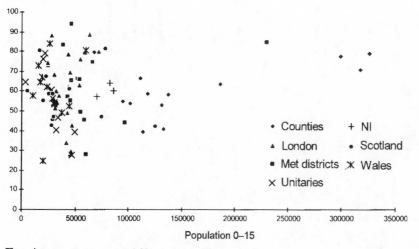

**Fig. A2.4**   *Percentage of children who are library members*

The graph in Figure A2.4 shows the percentage of children who are library members plotted against the total child population, for 86 authorities which supplied both figures. The Corporation of London has been omitted, as have two other authorities reporting percentages greater than 100.

## Collection development

### Q 19 & 20 Written policy documents and collection statements

|  | % of respondents with | | | |
|  | Policy document | Number of respondents | Collection statement | Number of respondents |
| --- | --- | --- | --- | --- |
| Counties | 65 | 23 | 18 | 22 |
| Metropolitan districts | 58 | 24 | 14 | 21 |
| London | 44 | 25 | 0 | 25 |
| Unitary authorities | 58 | 19 | 17 | 18 |
| Wales | 35 | 20 | 0 | 20 |
| Scotland | 28 | 25 | 4 | 25 |
| NI | 25 | 4 | 25 | 4 |
| UK | 47 | 140 | 9 | 135 |

### Q 21 Print-based resources (see also Figs A2.5 and A2.6)

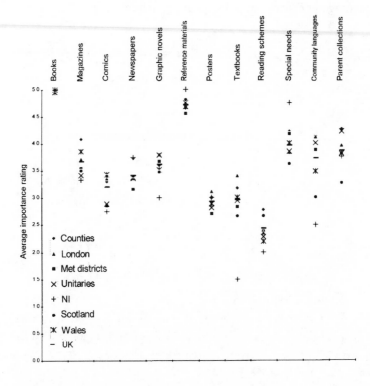

**Fig. A2.5** *Print-based resources: average importance rating*

Average importance ratings by provision of resources, UK as a whole

| | Magazines | Comics | News-papers | Graphic novels | Reference materials | Posters | Text-books | Reading schemes | Comm-unity languages | Parent collec-tions |
|---|---|---|---|---|---|---|---|---|---|---|
| Provide | 3.9 | 3.8 | 3.6 | 3.7 | 4.7 | 3.3 | 3.9 | 3.6 | 4.4 | 4.3 |
| Do not provide | 3.4 | 3.0 | 2.9 | 3.0 | 5.0 | 2.4 | 2.4 | 2.3 | 3.6 | 3.0 |
| % provision | 73 | 37 | 79 | 83 | 98 | 66 | 44 | 22 | 63 | 70 |

All authorities provide books, so are not included in the table above. Only three authorities did not provide reference materials for children, and all rated this resource 5.

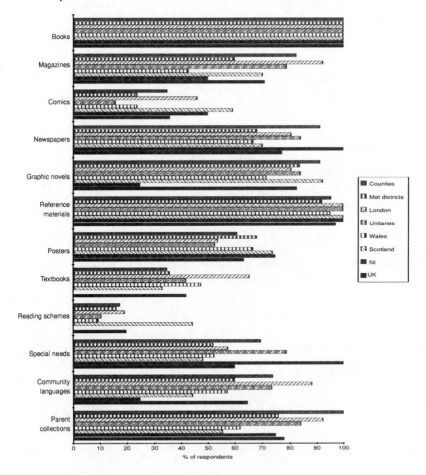

**Fig. A2.6**  *Percentage of libraries which provide each resource*

## Q22 & 23 Non-print-based and IT resources

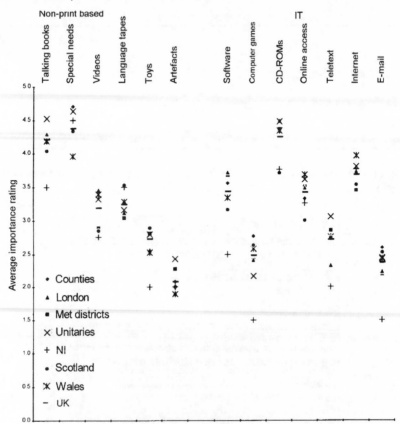

**Fig. A2.7**　*Non-print-based and IT resources: average importance rating*

*Average importance ratings by provision of resources, UK as a whole*

### Q 22 Non-print-based resources

|  | Talking books | Special needs | Videos | Language tapes | Toys | Artefacts |
|---|---|---|---|---|---|---|
| Provide | 4.3 | 4.6 | 3.3 | 3.4 | 3.2 | 3.4 |
| Do not provide | 2.8 | 4.3 | 2.8 | 2.6 | 2.3 | 2.1 |
| % provision | 97 | 69 | 80 | 83 | 51 | 5 |

## Q 23 IT resources

| | Software | Computer games | CD-ROM | Online access | Teletext | Internet | E-mail |
|---|---|---|---|---|---|---|---|
| Provide | 3.8 | 3.1 | 4.3 | 4.1 | 3.2 | 4.0 | 3.0 |
| Do not provide | 3.3 | 2.4 | 4.3 | 3.3 | 2.6 | 3.6 | 2.4 |
| % provision | 29 | 16 | 72 | 29 | 17 | 36 | 6 |

A factor analysis was carried out on the ratings from questions Q21 to Q23 combined (using the data from the UK as a whole). Six factors were extracted, accounting for approximately two-thirds of the variability in the data. These can be described as follows:

- *non-traditional resources* – magazines, comics, newspapers, software, computer games, teletext, e-mail, special needs talking books, language teaching tapes, toys, artefacts
- *AV and electronic resources* – talking books, videos, software, CD-ROM, online databases, Internet
- *special print collections* – material for children with disabilities, community language collections, parent/carer collections
- *visual materials* – magazines, comics, graphic novels, posters, toys and games
- *education* – national curriculum materials, reading schemes
- *traditional* – books, reference materials.

Whilst there were considerable variations in the factor scores between individual authorities, there were few observable differences between the sector averages:

- London was above average on the *education* factor
- the English unitary authorities were above average on the *AV* factor
- Scotland was below average on the *AV* factor.

Northern Ireland was not considered separately, as only two authorities supplied complete data for all three questions.

(Below-average factor scores indicate that the elements which are most important in that factor are rated as less important by that group on average than the average for the UK as a whole. Conversely, above-average factor scores indicate that the elements contributing most to those factors are rated as more important by that group than the average for the UK as a whole.)

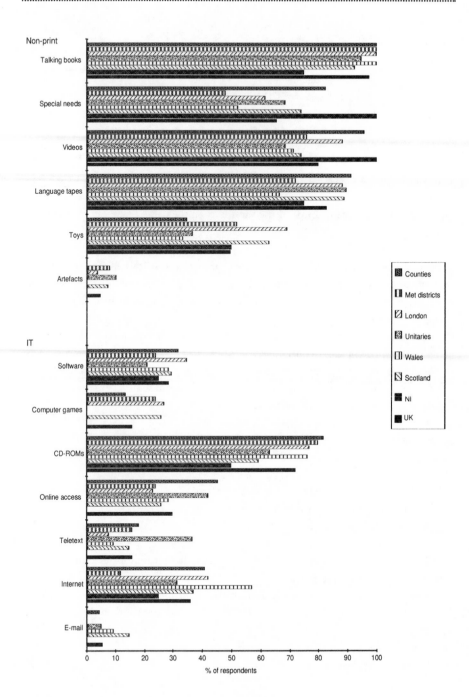

**Fig. A2.8**   *Percentage of libraries which provide each resource*

Q 24 Selection sources

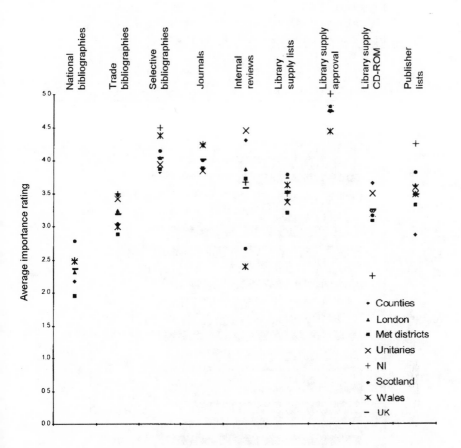

**Fig. A2.9**   *Selection sources: average importance rating*

Two categories of 'other' were also allowed. The data file contained no information as to what was included. Only 13 respondents used the first and three the second so they have been excluded from this and the following graph.

Average importance ratings by use of sources, UK as a whole

|  | National biblio- graphies | Trade biblio- graphies | Selective biblio graphies | Journals | Internal reviews | Library supply lists | Library supply approval | Library supply CD-ROM | Publisher lists |
|---|---|---|---|---|---|---|---|---|---|
| Use | 2.7 | 3.4 | 4.1 | 4.0 | 4.4 | 3.7 | 4.9 | 3.9 | 3.6 |
| Do not use | 2.0 | 2.4 | 3.5 | 3.8 | 2.9 | 2.7 | 4.0 | 3.1 | 3.1 |
| % use | 61 | 80 | 92 | 94 | 58 | 87 | 85 | 36 | 89 |

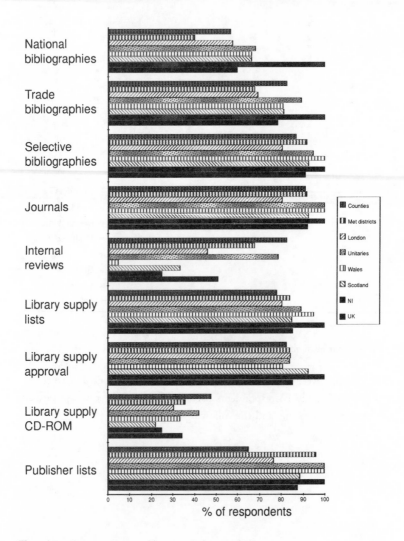

**Fig. A2.10**  *Percentage of libraries which use each resource*

Factor analysis on this question (excluding the 'other' categories) produced three factors, accounting for nearly two-thirds of the variance in the data:

- *lists* – all types of bibliography, journals, both types of catalogue
- *internal reviews*, approval collections
- *approval CD-ROM.*

Looking at the average factor scores by sector, Scotland was above average on the *lists* factor and the English counties below average. English counties and unitary authorities were above average on the second factor, with Wales and Scotland below average. Northern Ireland was below average on the *CD-ROM* factor.

(Below-average factor scores indicate that the elements which are most important in that factor are rated as less important by that group on average than the average for the UK as a whole. Conversely, above-average factor scores indicate that the elements contributing most to those factors are rated as more important by that group than the average for the UK as a whole.)

## Q 25 Stock selectors

Percentage of respondents where stock selection is mainly carried out by:

|  | Professional children's librarians | General professional librarians | Para-professionals | Other | Number of respondents |
|---|---|---|---|---|---|
| Counties | 91 | 39 | 0 | 0 | 23 |
| Metropolitan districts | 80 | 72 | 24 | 4 | 25 |
| London | 81 | 42 | 15 | 0 | 26 |
| Unitaries | 90 | 47 | 11 | 5 | 19 |
| Wales | 76 | 76 | 29 | 0 | 21 |
| Scotland | 89 | 54 | 32 | 0 | 28 |
| NI | 50 | 75 | 25 | 0 | 4 |
| UK | 84 | 56 | 19 | 1 | 146 |

## Q 26 Percentage of library services where selection is constrained by library suppliers

|  | % | Number of respondents |
|---|---|---|
| Counties | 26 | 23 |
| Metropolitan districts | 24 | 25 |
| London | 12 | 26 |
| Unitary authorities | 16 | 19 |
| Wales | 19 | 21 |
| Scotland | 19 | 27 |
| NI | 25 | 4 |
| UK | 19 | 145 |

## Q 27 Percentage of library services offering interlibrary loans

|  | % | Number of respondents |
|---|---|---|
| Counties | 87 | 23 |
| Metropolitan districts | 65 | 23 |
| London | 57 | 26 |
| Unitary authorities | 84 | 19 |
| Wales | 90 | 19 |
| Scotland | 60 | 25 |
| NI | 50 | 4 |
| UK | 72 | 139 |

## Q 28 Specific teenage collections

Only one library in Scotland did not provide a specific teenage collection. The graph in Figure A2.11 shows where these collections are housed (percentages of respondents).

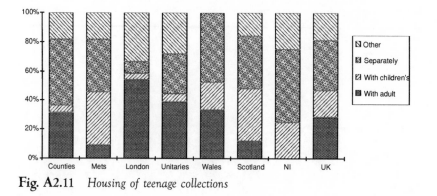

**Fig. A2.11**   *Housing of teenage collections*

## Access

Q 29 Means of access available to children and teenagers

Percentage of authorities reporting each:

| | Counties | Met districts | London | Unit-aries | Wales | Scotland | NI | UK |
|---|---|---|---|---|---|---|---|---|
| *Adult collection* | | | | | | | | |
| Card catalogue | 9 | 16 | 8 | 16 | 20 | 41 | 25 | 19 |
| OPAC | 65 | 76 | 96 | 53 | 70 | 56 | 75 | 70 |
| Internal indexes | 65 | 40 | 69 | 68 | 25 | 30 | 0 | 48 |
| Internal book lists | 65 | 48 | 46 | 53 | 20 | 41 | 25 | 45 |
| Multimedia | 4 | 4 | 8 | 5 | 0 | 0 | 0 | 4 |
| Published guides | 48 | 28 | 35 | 32 | 20 | 19 | 25 | 30 |
| Other | 35 | 0 | 0 | 53 | 10 | 7 | 75 | 17 |
| Average no of means available | 2.9 | 2.1 | 2.6 | 2.8 | 1.7 | 1.9 | 2.3 | 2.3 |
| | | | | | | | | |
| *Children's collection* | | | | | | | | |
| Card catalogue | 9 | 16 | 8 | 16 | 15 | 41 | 0 | 17 |
| OPAC | 65 | 72 | 96 | 53 | 65 | 59 | 75 | 69 |
| Internal indexes | 78 | 76 | 81 | 90 | 45 | 56 | 0 | 69 |
| Internal book lists | 83 | 72 | 58 | 58 | 25 | 59 | 50 | 60 |
| Multimedia | 22 | 8 | 8 | 5 | 0 | 0 | 0 | 7 |
| Published guides | 57 | 44 | 50 | 53 | 25 | 22 | 25 | 41 |
| Other | 35 | 0 | 0 | 47 | 10 | 7 | 75 | 17 |
| Average no of means available | 3.5 | 2.9 | 3.0 | 3.2 | 1.8 | 2.4 | 2.3 | 2.8 |
| No of respondents | 23 | 25 | 26 | 19 | 20 | 27 | 4 | 144 |

Q 30 Picture books (See Figures A2.12 and A2.13)

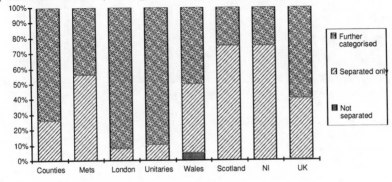

**Fig. A2.12**   *Percentage of all respondents*

The graph in Figure A2.13 shows the percentages of those authorities which further categorize picture books in each sector using each of the five systems specified in the questionnaire. Northern Ireland has not been shown, as only one authority further categorized picture books, although it is included in the total UK figures. The number of authorities included is given in italics.

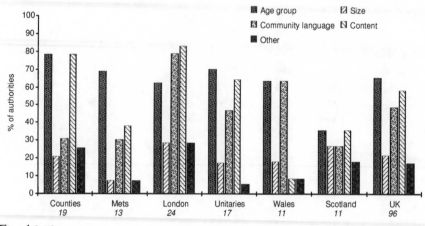

Fig. A2.13

## Q 31 Categorization of children's fiction

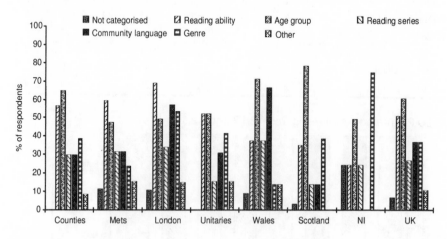

Fig. A2.14   *Percentage of all respondents*

## Q 32 Categorization of children's non-fiction

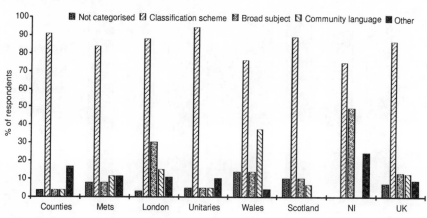

**Fig. A2.15**  *Percentage of all respondents*

## Q 33 & 34 Integration of children's materials

|  | % of respondents integrating | | | |
|---|---|---|---|---|
|  | Fiction& non-fiction | Number of respondents | Adult & children's non-fiction | Number of respondents |
| Counties | 13 | 23 | 35 | 23 |
| Metropolitan districts | 16 | 25 | 8 | 25 |
| London | 31 | 26 | 15 | 26 |
| Unitary authorities | 26 | 19 | 37 | 19 |
| Wales | 14 | 21 | 14 | 21 |
| Scotland | 18 | 28 | 26 | 27 |
| NI | 50 | 4 | 25 | 4 |
| UK | 21 | 146 | 22 | 145 |

## Q 35 Benefits of categorization

The graph in Figure A2.16 shows the percentage of respondents which believe that categorization benefits users in given ways and which believe it has no benefit. The total number of responses on which the figures are based is given in italics.

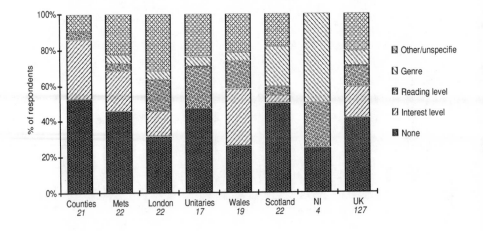

**Fig. A2.16**

## Promotion

### Q 36 & 37 Marketing and promotion

|  | General strategy | Number of respondents | Specific policies | Number of respondents |
|---|---|---|---|---|
| Counties | 26 | 23 | 48 | 23 |
| Metropolitan districts | 21 | 24 | 17 | 24 |
| London | 31 | 26 | 23 | 26 |
| Unitary authorities | 11 | 18 | 33 | 18 |
| Wales | 35 | 20 | 14 | 21 |
| Scotland | 24 | 25 | 26 | 27 |
| NI | 0 | 4 | 25 | 4 |
| UK | 24 | 140 | 27 | 143 |

Very few authorities responded to the supplementary parts of Q 37. For the UK as a whole, of 36 authorities which reported having specific promotional policies, and which completed the supplementary question, 50% indicated that their children's promotional policies were part of an overall strategy. Thirty-one authorities with no specific policy responded to the second supplementary, all indicating that such policies were *not* part of a more general strategy either.

### Q 38–40 Potential contribution of various activities to promotion

These three questions can be seen to be related, in that all are concerned with the promotion of children's reading. The average rating by sector on each item and the percentages of authorities providing each are given below for each question separately. Factor analyses were carried out on the data, but the results were far from conclusive. With data from all three questions combined, ten factors were extracted, but the main elements contributing to each seemed to have little in common with each other. Elements from questions 38 and 39 were intermixed in seven of the factors, two related to the specific promotional activities of Q40, and one was based on items from Q38 alone. It is impossible to give simple descriptions of more than a few of these factors. Each question was then considered separately, but this gave results which in part contradicted those of the combined analysis.

### Q 38 Potential contribution of in-house activities to promotion

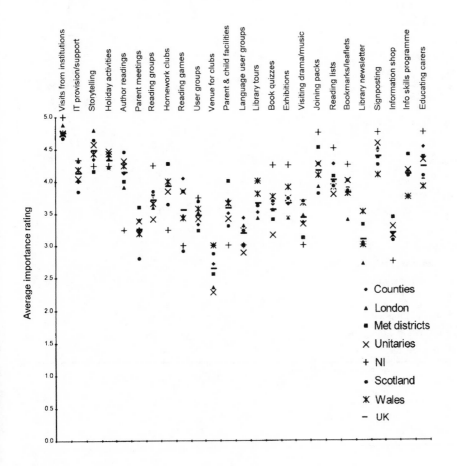

**Fig. A2.17**    *Average importance rating of each activity*

Eight authorities made an entry in the 'other' category, giving an average rating of 4.6 (although the items rated may not be the same). These have not been included in the graphs in Figures A2.17 and A2.18.

### Average importance ratings by provision of activities, UK as a whole

|  | Authorities which provide | Authorities which do not provide | % providing |
|---|---|---|---|
| Visits from institutions | 4.7 | 5.0 | 98 |
| IT provision/support | 4.4 | 3.8 | 57 |
| Storytelling | 4.6 | 3.9 | 90 |
| Holiday activities | 4.4 | 3.6 | 95 |
| Author readings | 4.3 | 3.3 | 88 |
| Parent meetings | 4.0 | 3.2 | 19 |
| Reading groups | 4.1 | 3.6 | 27 |
| Homework clubs | 4.3 | 3.9 | 27 |
| Reading games | 4.2 | 3.0 | 50 |
| User groups | 4.5 | 3.3 | 22 |
| Venue for clubs | 3.6 | 2.7 | 4 |
| Parent & child facilities | 3.9 | 3.4 | 36 |
| Language user groups | 4.1 | 3.1 | 17 |
| Library tours | 3.9 | 3.2 | 66 |
| Book quizzes | 3.8 | 3.0 | 73 |
| Exhibitions | 3.8 | 2.9 | 84 |
| Visiting drama/music | 3.9 | 2.9 | 60 |
| Joining packs | 4.3 | 4.1 | 49 |
| Reading lists | 4.1 | 3.8 | 69 |
| Bookmarks/leaflets | 3.9 | 3.3 | 84 |
| Library newsletter | 3.7 | 3.1 | 14 |
| Signposting | 4.5 | 3.7 | 86 |
| Information shop | 4.0 | 3.2 | 10 |
| Information skills programme | 4.5 | 3.7 | 60 |
| Educating carers | 4.6 | 3.8 | 64 |

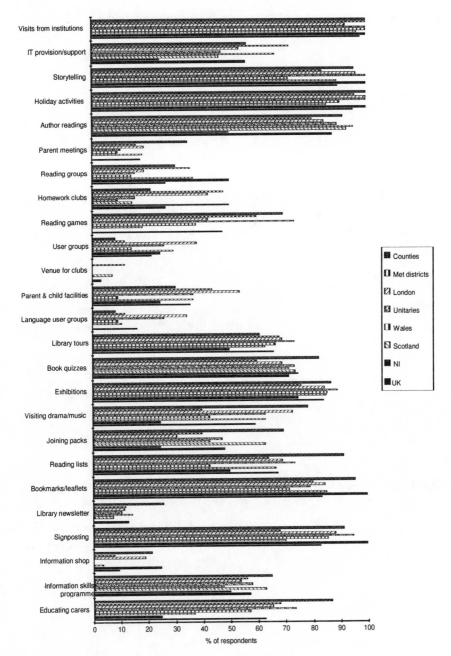

**Fig. A2.18**   *Percentage of authorities providing each activity*

## Q 39 Potential contribution of external activities to promotion

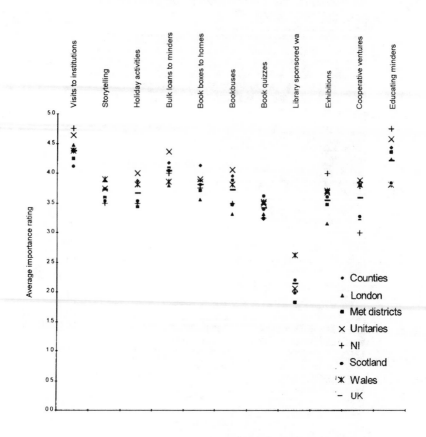

**Fig. A2.19**   *Average importance rating of each activity*

Nine authorities made an entry under 'other', included in the graph in Figure A2.20. The average rating was 4.1, but the details of the activity being rated were not on the file.

## Average importance ratings by provision of activities, UK as a whole

| | Visits to institutions | Story- telling | Holiday activity | Bulk loans | Book boxes | Book buses | Book quizzes | Walks | Exhib- itions | Coop ventures | Educ minders |
|---|---|---|---|---|---|---|---|---|---|---|---|
| Provide | 4.5 | 4.1 | 4.1 | 4.4 | 4.3 | 4.3 | 3.9 | 3.5 | 3.8 | 4.3 | 4.5 |
| Do not provide | 3.8 | 3.5 | 3.1 | 3.5 | 3.5 | 3.6 | 3.2 | 2.1 | 3.2 | 3.4 | 3.6 |
| % provision | 90 | 36 | 57 | 64 | 39 | 21 | 37 | 6 | 59 | 30 | 70 |

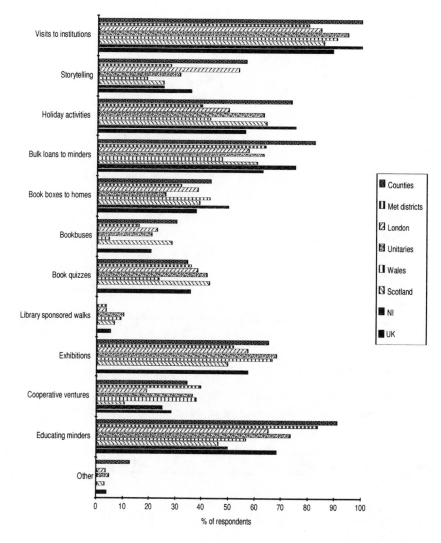

**Fig. A2.20**  *Percentage of authorities providing each activity*

Q 40 Potential contribution of promotional activities to promotion

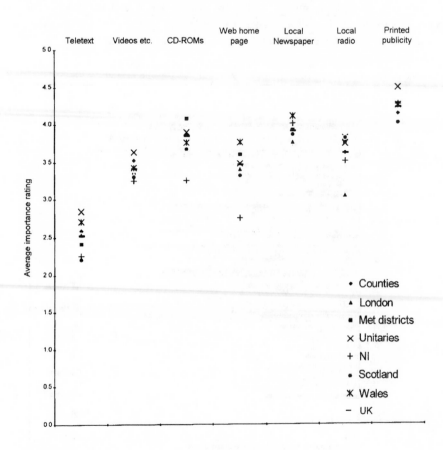

**Fig. A2.21**    *Average importance rating of each activity*

Nine authorities made an entry under 'other', included in the graph in Figure A2.22. The average rating was 3.9, but the details of the activity being rated were not on the file.

Average importance ratings by provision of activities, UK as a whole

|  | Teletext | Videos | CD-ROM | Web home page | Local paper | Local radio | Printed publicity |
|---|---|---|---|---|---|---|---|
| Provide | 2.6 | 3.7 | 4.3 | 3.8 | 4.0 | 3.9 | 4.3 |
| Do not provide | 2.6 | 3.2 | 3.5 | 3.4 | 3.8 | 3.4 | 4.1 |
| % provision | 8 | 42 | 42 | 26 | 70 | 38 | 84 |

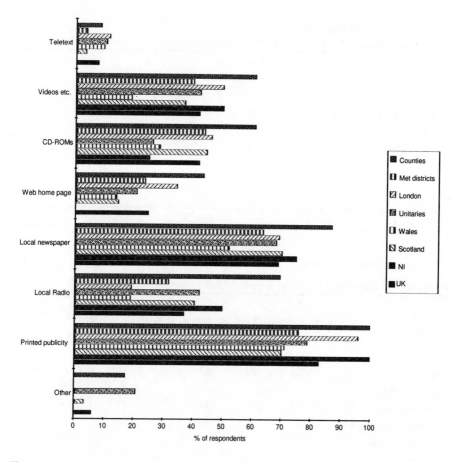

**Fig. A2.22**  *Percentage of authorities providing each activity*

## Q 41 Specific support for activities
Percentage of authorities offering specific support for the following activities

|  | Counties | Met districts | London | Unitaries | Wales | Scotland | NI | UK |
|---|---|---|---|---|---|---|---|---|
| Paired reading | 0 | 12 | 0 | 0 | 5 | 23 | 25 | 8 |
| Family reading groups | 32 | 24 | 19 | 17 | 24 | 12 | 0 | 20 |
| Teenage reading groups | 14 | 8 | 8 | 0 | 5 | 4 | 0 | 6 |
| Bookstart projects | 46 | 44 | 19 | 33 | 5 | 19 | 0 | 27 |
| Homework | 59 | 72 | 58 | 56 | 29 | 35 | 75 | 52 |
| Other | 18 | 8 | 8 | 11 | 14 | 0 | 0 | 9 |
| No of respondents | 22 | 25 | 26 | 18 | 21 | 26 | 4 | 142 |

## Q 42 Evaluation of activities
Percentage of authorities undertaking evaluation

|  | % | Number of respondents |
|---|---|---|
| Counties | 18 | 22 |
| Metropolitan districts | 33 | 24 |
| London | 23 | 26 |
| Unitary authorities | 21 | 19 |
| Wales | 11 | 19 |
| Scotland | 35 | 20 |
| NI | 0 | 3 |
| UK | 23 | 133 |

## Q 43 Partnership schemes

Percentage of authorities engaging in partnership schemes

|  | Counties | Met districts | London | Unitaries | Wales | Scotland | NI | UK |
|---|---|---|---|---|---|---|---|---|
| Other library authorities | 57 | 40 | 58 | 63 | 43 | 31 | 100 | 49 |
| Other local authority depts | 83 | 56 | 62 | 63 | 48 | 35 | 0 | 56 |
| Teachers/schools | 96 | 68 | 77 | 74 | 71 | 77 | 100 | 78 |
| Other professional/ voluntary groups | 65 | 48 | 42 | 58 | 43 | 50 | 50 | 51 |
| Publishers | 65 | 40 | 46 | 32 | 29 | 39 | 0 | 41 |
| National bodies | 22 | 8 | 19 | 5 | 19 | 58 | 0 | 22 |
| Parent groups | 13 | 12 | 15 | 21 | 19 | 31 | 25 | 19 |
| Other | 13 | 20 | 19 | 32 | 0 | 4 | 0 | 14 |
| No of respondents | 23 | 25 | 26 | 19 | 21 | 26 | 4 | 144 |

## Q 44 External funding

Percentage of authorities receiving external funding

| | Counties | Met districts | London | Unitaries | Wales | Scotland | NI | UK |
|---|---|---|---|---|---|---|---|---|
| European Union | 8.7 | 0 | 0 | 5 | 0 | 0 | 0 | 2 |
| Lottery | 4 | 4 | 0 | 5 | 0 | 0 | 0 | 2 |
| Local government | 13 | 36 | 12 | 21 | 5 | 4 | 0 | 15 |
| Other council depts | 17 | 24 | 35 | 42 | 24 | 15 | 0 | 25 |
| Local business | 61 | 40 | 31 | 37 | 19 | 42 | 25 | 38 |
| Local service organizations | 13 | 0 | 8 | 5 | 5 | 8 | 25 | 7 |
| Arts council | 30 | 4 | 15 | 26 | 52 | 81 | 75 | 36 |
| Regional arts boards | 57 | 32 | 8 | 26 | 10 | 0 | 0 | 21 |
| Other | 22 | 12 | 8 | 16 | 5 | 4 | 0 | 10 |
| No of respondents | 23 | 25 | 26 | 19 | 21 | 26 | 4 | 144 |

## Service assessment

### Q 45 Percentage of children's library services using performance indicators

| | % | Number of respondents |
|---|---|---|
| Counties | 50 | 20 |
| Metropolitan districts | 27 | 22 |
| London | 56 | 25 |
| Unitary authorities | 47 | 19 |
| Wales | 33 | 21 |
| Scotland | 27 | 22 |
| NI | 25 | 4 |
| UK | 40 | 133 |

### Q 46 Provision by age group (See Figure A2.23)

A factor analysis was carried out on these data and four factors were identified:

- *collection* – all categories except those aged 5 or more not in school in terms of the total collection
- *primary promotion* – promotional activities for pre-school children and those aged 5 to 11
- *secondary promotion* – promotional activities for children aged 12 to 16
- *no school* – children aged over 5 not in school in terms of the total collection and promotional activities.

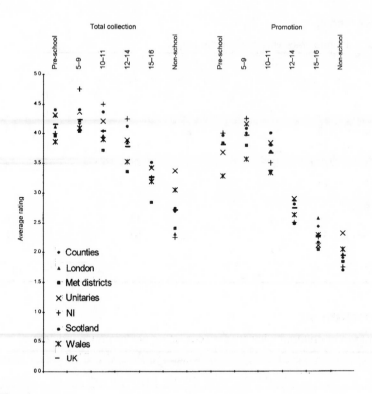

**Fig. A2.23**

Standardized average factor scores were calculated for each sector. The metropolitan districts were below the UK average on the *collection* and *secondary promotion* factors. London was above average on both *promotion* factors. The unitary authorities were above average on the *no school* factor. Wales was below average on the *primary promotion* factor and above average on the *no school* factor. Scotland was above average on the *collection* factor. Northern Ireland was above average on the *collection* factor and below average on the *no school* factor.

Because of the superficial similarity between questions 13 and 46, data from both were combined for a further factor analysis. This gave no new insights, however. The eight factors extracted were similar to those found when each question was considered separately, with the exception of the items relating to children over five not in school, which grouped together to form a single factor.

## Q 47 Training

All graphs show the percentage of respondents in each category, based on those authorities replying to both parts of the question. The numbers included vary:

| | |
|---|---|
| Counties | 17–21 |
| Metropolitan districts | 22–5 |
| London | 20–5 |
| Unitary authorities | 16–19 |
| Wales | 19–20 |
| Scotland | 22–7 |
| Northern Ireland | 4 |
| UK | 124–39 |

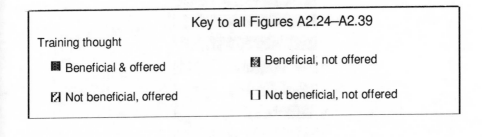

**Key to all Figures A2.24–A2.39**

Training thought

■ Beneficial & offered          ▨ Beneficial, not offered

▨ Not beneficial, offered          ☐ Not beneficial, not offered

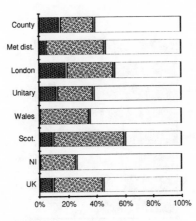

**Fig. A2.24**   *Teaching*

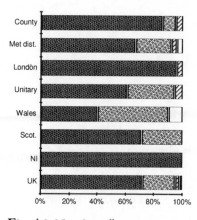

**Fig. A2.25**    *Storytelling*

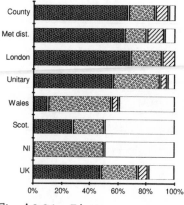

**Fig. A2.26**    *Ethnicity*

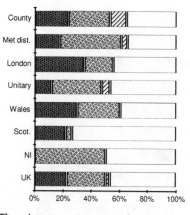

**Fig. A2.27**    *Community languages*

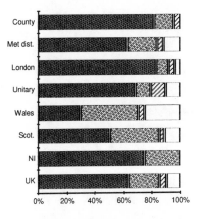

**Fig. A2.28**   *Selection*

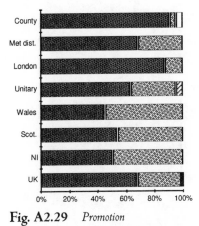

**Fig. A2.29**   *Promotion*

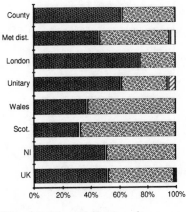

**Fig. A2.30**   *Children's reading*

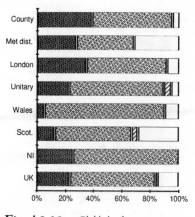

**Fig. A2.31**　*Child development*

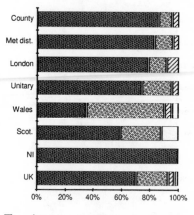

**Fig. A2.32**　*Disability*

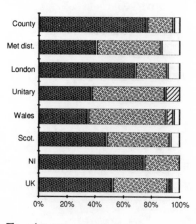

**Fig. A2.33**　*Activities*

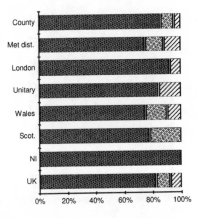

**Fig. A2.34**    *Customer care*

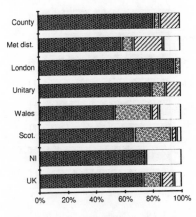

**Fig. A2.35**    *Management*

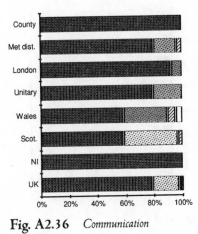

**Fig. A2.36**    *Communication*

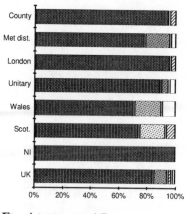

**Fig. A2.37**  *IT skills*

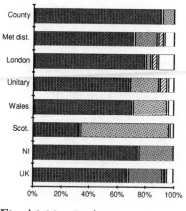

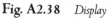

**Fig. A2.38**  *Display*

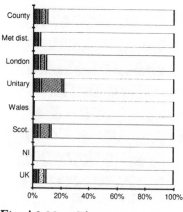

**Fig. A2.39**  *Other*

# Index

# Outstanding Books for Children and Young People

## The LA guide to Carnegie/Greenaway winners 1937–1997

### KEITH BARKER

The Library Association's two children's book awards, the Carnegie Medal for outstanding writing for children, and the Kate Greenaway Medal for outstanding books in terms of illustration, are recognized the world over for their promotion of excellence in writing and illustration for children. The winners and commended books help to provide a microcosm of children's literature in the United Kingdom over the last half of the 20th century, and to identify trends, from forgotten writers and classics of the early period, through developments in the printing of illustrated material, to the gritty realism of recent winners.

Launched in the National Year of Reading, this book celebrates over 60 years of writing and illustration, and is introduced by a Foreword from the Rt Hon. David Blunkett MP, Secretary of State for Education and Employment. It presents a complete annotated list of winners, commended and highly commended titles, given in chronological order. The author supplies bibliographical details for each title, with ISBNs for those still in print, followed by a description of the story or illustration, and a critical evaluation of the book's relevance to today's children.

Of considerable historical interest, this list of outstanding titles also has immense validity today. It is intended as an essential desktop companion for children's librarians and teachers who will find this book an ideal collection or curriculum development tool. It will also be a useful reference work for researchers in children's literature, publishers, library school students studying children's literature, and parents wishing to choose excellent reading material for their children.

'Barker's book is an invaluable guide through the thickets of contemporary children's fiction'
*The Mail on Sunday*

1998; 152pp; paperback; 1-85604-287-1; £15.95

# Managing Library Services for Children and Young People
a practical handbook

## CATHERINE BLANSHARD

In the light of the current financial climate of cutbacks and competing priorities, it is becoming increasingly important to review children's and youth services in order to make them relevant and marketable to their audience, and to attract funding and sponsorship for the service.

This practical handbook shows how library managers can make use of ideas taken from current business practice to evaluate and assess the library service, and how this can result in value and quality being added to the services offered.

This text answers a real need for a hands-on manual for the practitioner in this sector. Emphasizing that the needs of the child and of the young person should drive management decisions, it demonstrates how these can best be addressed by the implementation of service specifications, business plans, targets, profiles and strategies.

Dealing with such diverse areas as: finding out what children want, display and promotion, measuring quality, and providing a young peoples' information strategy, this accessible handbook provides service managers with a manual of best practice within each area of the service, including:

- managing change
- the users of children's libraries
- managing the children's service
- managing performance
- strategic management
- key service issues
- stock related issues.

This book is essential reading for service managers in public libraries, senior managers in local government, school librarians, governors and teachers and all those concerned with the provision of library services to children and young people.

'This is a highly practical, hard-headed management text which must be essential reading for all those who have a role to play in a provision for library and information services for children and youth'

*Library Management*

1998; 208pp hardback; 1-85604-226-X; £37.50